BARTLETT'S
WORDS TO
LIVE BY

·◆·

THE BARTLETT'S LIBRARY

Bartlett's Familiar Quotations, Seventeenth Edition
Bartlett's Book of Anecdotes
Bartlett's Roget's Thesaurus
Bartlett's Poems for Occasions
Bartlett's Bible Quotations
Bartlett's Shakespeare Quotations
Bartlett's Words to Live By

BARTLETT'S
WORDS TO
LIVE BY

ADVICE AND INSPIRATION
FOR EVERYDAY LIFE

•◆•

Foreword by Kurt Vonnegut

Little, Brown and Company
NEW YORK   BOSTON   LONDON

Little, Brown and Company
Hachette Book Group USA
237 Park Avenue, New York, NY 10017

Visit our Web site at www.HachetteBookGroupUSA.com.

First Edition: May 2006

The quotations in this book are from *Bartlett's Familiar Quotations,* Seventeenth Edition, Justin Kaplan, General Editor.

Library of Congress Cataloging-in-Publication Data

Bartlett's words to live by : advice and inspiration for everyday life /
   John Bartlett. — 1st ed.
     p. cm.
   "The quotations in this book are from Bartlett's familiar quotations,
seventeenth edition, Justin Kaplan, general editor" — T.p. verso.
   ISBN 978-0-316-01624-7 (hc)
   1. Conduct of life — Quotations, maxims, etc.   I. Bartlett, John,
1820–1905. Familiar quotations.   II. Title: Words to live by.

PN6084.C556B37 2006
808.88'2 — dc22   2005035737

10 9 8 7 6 5 4 3 2

Q-FF

Printed in the United States of America

Contents

Foreword

•◆•

ANY LIST OF GREAT AMERICAN INVENTORS, the Wright brothers
and Thomas Edison, and the African-American communities that
gave the world the remedy for depression and despair they
called "the blues," and on and on, should surely include John
Bartlett (1830–1905), of Boston. In 1855 he created and published the world's first book of the sort you hold in your hands
now, a compendium of short and pithy excerpts from the writ-
ings or speeches of some of the smartest or at least most famous
or notorious people who ever lived.

Having mentioned your hands, though, let me call your at-
tention to the pleasant heft of the book, almost like that of a kit-
ten or puppy, and the dainty signals it sends to your brain from
your sensitive fingertips as you turn its pages. My point: Not just
this book, but any book of similar size, is flirtatious with your
body, which a computer is not. And, in an age of frenzied worship of electronics, try this for a miracle: Open this or any book
absolutely anywhere above water, and as long as there is any
light at all, it will talk to you! And not even the FBI can listen in!
Talk about privacy!

Listen: As ancient and primitive in design a book may be, as
unelectronic, as made of nothing but products of the fields and
woodlands, its continued successes as a means of storage and

retrieval of information entitle it to celebration by us all as one hell of an invention. So let us give it a razzmatazz, high-tech name, since it works so well in 2006. Why not "OMA," for "Open Me Anywhere"?

This particular OMA, and it is a honey, is intended by its editors to be a search engine, or "Easter egg hunt," if you like, for persons "whose name is Legion" (St. Mark 5:9), hungering for inspirational or at least comforting soundbites from the past. Find here 1,400 "Easter eggs," so to speak, culled from the 25,000 for simply anybody in the seventeenth edition of *Bartlett's Familiar Quotations,* which, according to my bathroom scale, weighs four pounds and change.

My own favorite Easter egg? It isn't just for alcoholics, although it is famous as a treasure for recovering alcoholics. Nor am I an alcoholic, luckily enough, a matter not of character but of genes. "There but for the Grace of God go I" (Anonymous). So here goes:

"God, give us grace to accept with serenity the things that cannot be changed, courage to change the things which should be changed, and the wisdom to distinguish the one from the other."

Kerpow.

This was said in 1943 by the American theologian Reinhold Niebuhr (1892–1971), simply as a part of a sermon on Cape Cod, I'm told. No big deal, he thought. But it was almost as though Albert Einstein (1879–1955) had been playing his fiddle and suddenly heard himself say, "Energy equals mass times the speed of light squared." And Niebuhr's prayer does indeed have a similar mathematical clarity. I put that prayer into a novel of mine, incidentally, which was published in what used to be the Soviet Union. I am told that thousands of people there were thunderstruck by its good sense and copied it out and put it up on a wall or whatever. And communism went bust.

As for advice or inspiration from parents instead of an OMA: William Shakespeare (1564–1616) makes fun in act one, scene three of *Hamlet* of how sententiously useless such advice can be, with the windbag Polonius intoning, "Neither a borrower, nor a lender be," and on and on.

The only advice I ever got from my own father, God rest his soul, was, "Take your hands out of your pockets and stand up straight."

"Easier said than done" (Anonymous).

KURT VONNEGUT

Editor's note: The quotations in this book are arranged chronologically within each chapter.

BARTLETT'S WORDS TO LIVE BY

Adversity

A merry heart maketh a cheerful countenance: but by
sorrow of the heart the spirit is broken.

The Bible, The Proverbs

The meek shall inherit the earth.

The Bible, The Book of Psalms

Oh that I had wings like a dove! for then
would I fly away, and be at rest.

The Bible, The Book of Psalms

The ear of jealousy heareth all things.

The Bible, The Apocrypha, The Wisdom of Solomon

Many are in high place, and of renown:
but mysteries are revealed unto the meek.

*The Bible, The Apocrypha, The Wisdom of Jesus the
Son of Sirach, or Ecclesiasticus*

Yet a little while is the light with you. Walk while
ye have the light, lest darkness come upon you.

The Bible, The Gospel According to Saint John

There is a strength in the union even of very sorry men.
Homer, Iliad

A small rock holds back a great wave.
Homer, Odyssey

The softest things in the world overcome the
hardest things in the world.
Lao-tzu, The Way of Lao-tzu

A journey of a thousand miles must begin with
a single step.
Lao-tzu, The Way of Lao-tzu

All men know the utility of useful things;
but they do not know the utility of futility.
Chuang-tzu, This Human World

Those who aim at great deeds must also suffer greatly.
Marcus Licinius Crassus, From Plutarch, Lives

Never find your delight in another's misfortune.
Publilius Syrus, Maxim

Fire is the test of gold; adversity, of strong men.
Lucius Annaeus Seneca, Moral Essays

Nothing happens to anybody which he is
not fitted by nature to bear.
Marcus Aurelius Antoninus, Meditations

He said not "Thou shalt not be tempested, thou shalt
not be travailed, thou shalt not be dis-eased";
but he said, "Thou shalt not be overcome."
Juliana of Norwich, Revelations of Divine Love

For he that naught n' assaieth, naught
n' acheveth.
Geoffrey Chaucer, Troilus and Criseyde

In the country of the blind the one-eyed man is king.
Desiderius Erasmus, Adagia

A hard beginning maketh a good ending.
John Heywood, Proverbs

Nothing is impossible to a willing heart.
John Heywood, Proverbs

Better is half a loaf than no bread.
John Heywood, Proverbs

In my end is my beginning.
Mary, Queen of Scots, Motto

Prosperity doth best discover vice, but adversity doth best
discover virtue.
Francis Bacon, Essays

Fight till the last gasp.
William Shakespeare, King Henry the Sixth, Part I

To fear the worst oft cures the worse.
William Shakespeare, Troilus and Cressida

The worst is not,
So long as we can say, "This is the worst."
William Shakespeare, King Lear

The way to bliss lies not on beds of down,
And he that had no cross deserves no crown.
Francis Quarles, Esther

When angry, count ten before you speak;
if very angry, an hundred.

Thomas Jefferson, A Decalogue of Canons for Observation in Practical Life

For I have been a man, and that
means to have been a fighter.

Johann Wolfgang von Goethe, Divan of East and West

Nothing, I am sure, calls forth the faculties so much as the
being obliged to struggle with the world.

Mary Wollstonecraft, Thoughts on the Education of Daughters

You write to me that it's impossible; the word is not French.

Napoleon I, Letter to General Lemarois

Look not thou down but up!

Robert Browning, Rabbi Ben Ezra

Out of the wreck I rise.

Robert Browning, Ixion

It's a mad world. Mad as Bedlam.

Charles Dickens, David Copperfield

The whole history of the progress of human liberty
shows that all concessions yet made to her august
claims have been born of earnest struggle. . . .
If there is no struggle, there is no progress.
Frederick Douglass, Speech at Canandaigua, New York

Mishaps are like knives, that either serve us or cut us,
as we grasp them by the blade or the handle.
James Russell Lowell, Literary Essays

The minority is always right.
Henrik Ibsen, An Enemy of the People

Simply by being compelled to keep constantly on
his guard, a man may grow so weak as to be
unable any longer to defend himself.
Friedrich Wilhelm Nietzsche, Ecce Homo

A man cannot be too careful in the choice of his enemies.
Oscar Wilde, The Picture of Dorian Gray

You can't hold a man down without staying down with him.
Booker T. Washington, Attributed

There is such a thing as a man being too proud to fight.
Woodrow Wilson, Address to Foreign-Born Citizens

When a just cause reaches its flood tide . . . whatever stands
in the way must fall before its overwhelming power.

Carrie Catt, Speech at Stockholm, Is Woman Suffrage Progressing?

The Promised Land always lies on the other side of a
wilderness.

Havelock Ellis, The Dance of Life

The humblest citizen of all the land, when clad in the armor
of a righteous cause, is stronger than all the hosts of Error.

*William Jennings Bryan, Speech at the
National Democratic Convention, Chicago*

Too long a sacrifice
Can make a stone of the heart.
O when may it suffice?

William Butler Yeats, Michael Robartes and the Dancer

Victory at all costs, victory in spite of all terror,
victory however long and hard the road may be;
for without victory there is no survival.

*Sir Winston Spencer Churchill, First Statement
as Prime Minister, House of Commons*

"Not in vain" may be the pride of those who have
survived and the epitaph of those who fell.

Sir Winston Spencer Churchill, Speech in the House of Commons

It is not enough to fight. It is the spirit which
we bring to the fight that decides the issue.
It is morale that wins the victory.

George C. Marshall, Military Review

I'll come to thee by moonlight,
though hell should bar the way.

Alfred Noyes, The Highwayman

No one can make you feel inferior without your consent.

Eleanor Roosevelt, This Is My Story

I long ago came to the conclusion that
all life is 6 to 5 against.

Damon Runyon, Money from Home

Fortunately [psycho]analysis is not the
only way to resolve inner conflicts. Life itself
still remains a very effective therapist.

Karen Horney, Our Inner Conflicts

We fight for lost causes because we know that our
defeat and dismay may be the preface to our
successors' victory, though that victory itself will be
temporary; we fight rather to keep something alive than
in the expectation that anything will triumph.

T. S. Eliot, For Lancelot Andrews

I believe that man will not merely endure: he will prevail.
William Faulkner, Speech upon receiving the Nobel Prize

A man can be destroyed but not defeated.
Ernest Hemingway, The Old Man and the Sea

In a dark time, the eye begins to see.
Theodore Roethke, In a Dark Time

In Italy for thirty years under the Borgias they had
warfare, terror, murder, bloodshed, but they produced
Michelangelo, Leonardo da Vinci, and the Renaissance. In
Switzerland they had brotherly love, they had
five hundred years of democracy and peace. And
what did that produce? The cuckoo-clock.
Orson Welles, Speech written into The Third Man

For of those to whom much is given, much is required. And
when at some future date the high court of history sits in
judgment on each of us, recording whether in our brief
span of service we fulfilled our responsibilities to the state,
our success or failure, in whatever office we hold, will be
measured by the answers to four questions: First, were we
truly men of courage . . . Second, were we truly men of
judgment . . . Third, were we truly men of integrity . . .
Finally, were we truly men of dedication?
John Fitzgerald Kennedy, Speech to the Massachusetts State Legislature

There is always inequity in life. Some men are killed in a war and some men are wounded, and some men never leave the country . . . Life is unfair.

John Fitzgerald Kennedy, Press conference

It ain't over till it's over.

Yogi Berra, Comment on National League pennant race

You may trod me in the very dirt
But still, like dust, I'll rise.

Maya Angelou, Still I Rise

You have to eat and keep going. Eating is a small, good thing in a time like this.

Raymond Carver, Cathedral

It's not that easy bein' green.

Sesame Street, Bein' Green, Sung by Kermit the Frog

We shall overcome, we shall overcome,
We shall overcome some day
Oh, deep in my heart I do believe
We shall overcome some day.

Anonymous, Adapted for the civil rights movement from an old religious song

You can't make an omelet without breaking eggs.

Anonymous, French proverb

Art and Beauty

Painting is silent poetry, and poetry painting that speaks.

Simonides, From Plutarch, De Gloria Atheniensium

Whatever is in any way beautiful hath its source of beauty
in itself, and is complete in itself; praise forms no part of it.
So it is none the worse nor the better for being praised.

Marcus Aurelius Antoninus, Meditations

Too late I loved you, O Beauty ever ancient and ever new!
Too late I loved you! And, behold, you were within me, and
I out of myself, and there I searched for you.

Saint Augustine, Confessions

If you have two loaves of bread,
sell one and buy a hyacinth.

Anonymous, Persian saying

There are Six Essentials in painting. The first is called spirit;
the second, rhythm; the third, thought; the fourth, scenery;
the fifth, the brush; and the last is the ink.

Ching Hao, Notes on Brushwork

Much is the force of heaven-bred poesy.

William Shakespeare, The Two Gentlemen of Verona

Beauty's but skin deep.

*John Davies of Hereford, A Select Second Husband
for Sir Thomas Overburie's Wife*

Art hath an enemy called Ignorance.

Ben Jonson, Every Man out of His Humour

Beauty stands
In the admiration only of weak minds
Led captive.

John Milton, Paradise Regained

What passion cannot Music raise and quell?

John Dryden, A Song for Saint Cecilia's Day

One and the same thing can at the same time be good, bad,
and indifferent, e.g., music is good to the melancholy, bad
to those who mourn, and neither good nor bad to the deaf.

Benedict Spinoza, Ethics

Choose an author as you choose a friend.

Wentworth Dillon, Earl of Roscommon, Essay on Translated Verse

Books, the children of the brain.
Jonathan Swift, A Tale of a Tub

Vision is the art of seeing things invisible.
Jonathan Swift, Thoughts on Various Subjects

Books are the legacies that a great genius leaves
to mankind, which are delivered down from
generation to generation, as presents to the
posterity of those who are yet unborn.
Joseph Addison, The Spectator

A true critic ought to dwell rather upon excellencies
than imperfections, to discover the concealed beauties
of a writer, and communicate to the world such
things as are worth their observation.
Joseph Addison, The Spectator

Criticism is easy, art is difficult.
Philippe Destouches, Le Glorieux

Women who are either indisputably beautiful, or
indisputably ugly, are best flattered upon the score
of their understandings; but those who are in a state
of mediocrity are best flattered upon their beauty, or
at least their graces; for every woman who is not
absolutely ugly thinks herself handsome.

Philip Dormer Stanhope, Earl of Chesterfield, Letters to His Son

Handsome is that handsome does.

Oliver Goldsmith, The Vicar of Wakefield

One ought, every day at least, to hear a little song,
read a good poem, see a fine picture, and, if it were
possible, to speak a few reasonable words.

Johann Wolfgang von Goethe, Wilhelm Meister's Apprenticeship

In art the best is good enough.

Johann Wolfgang von Goethe, Italian Journey

Individuality of expression is the
beginning and end of all art.

Johann Wolfgang von Goethe, Proverbs in Prose

Poetry fettered fetters the human race. Nations are
destroyed, or flourish, in proportion as their poetry,
painting, and music are destroyed or flourish!

William Blake, Jerusalem

Life is earnest, art is gay.

Johann Friedrich von Schiller, Wallenstein's Camp

Art! Who comprehends her? With whom can one
consult concerning this great goddess?

Ludwig van Beethoven, Letter to Bettina von Arnim

Beauty without grace is the hook without the bait.

Ralph Waldo Emerson, The Conduct of Life

Every genuine work of art has as much reason for being as
the earth and the sun.

Ralph Waldo Emerson, Society and Solitude

You know who the critics are? The men
who have failed in literature and art.

Benjamin Disraeli, Earl of Beaconsfield, Lothair

Art for art's sake is an empty phrase. Art for the sake
of the true, art for the sake of the good and the
beautiful, that is the faith I am searching for.

George Sand, Letter to Alexandre Saint-Jean

All good things which exist are the fruits of originality.

John Stuart Mill, On Liberty

Of all the needs a book has, the chief
need is that it be readable.

Anthony Trollope, An Autobiography

The perception of beauty is a moral test.

Henry David Thoreau, Journal

Remember that the most beautiful things in the world are
the most useless; peacocks and lilies for instance.

John Ruskin, The Stones of Venice

All great art is the work of the whole living creature,
body and soul, and chiefly of the soul.

John Ruskin, The Stones of Venice

Life without industry is guilt, industry
without art is brutality.

John Ruskin, Lectures on Art

To have great poets, there must be great audiences, too.

Walt Whitman, Collect

One must not always think that feeling is everything.
Art is nothing without form.

Gustave Flaubert, Letter to Madame Louise Colet

Art is a human activity having for its purpose the
transmission to others of the highest and
best feelings to which men have risen.

Leo Nikolaevich Tolstoi, What Is Art?

If you want a golden rule that will fit everybody, this is it:
Have nothing in your houses that you do not know
to be useful, or believe to be beautiful.

William Morris, The Beauty of Life

Art should be independent of all claptrap — should stand
alone, and appeal to the artistic sense of eye or ear,
without confounding this with emotions entirely
foreign to it, as devotion, pity, love, patriotism, and
the like. All these have no kind of concern with it.

James McNeill Whistler, The Gentle Art of Making Enemies

The mortality of all inanimate things is terrible to me,
but that of books most of all.

William Dean Howells, Letter to Charles Eliot Norton

Right now a moment of time is fleeting by! Capture its
reality in paint! To do that we must put all else out of
our minds. We must become that moment, make
ourselves a sensitive recording plate . . . give the
image of what we actually see, forgetting everything
that has been seen before our time.

Paul Cézanne, From Joachim Gasquet, Paul Cézanne

Art comes to you proposing frankly to give nothing but the
highest quality to your moments as they pass.

Walter Pater, Studies in the History of the Renaissance

You don't make a poem with ideas, but with words.

Stéphane Mallarmé, From Paul Valéry, Degas, Danse, Dessin

It is art that makes life, makes interest, makes importance,
for our consideration and application of these things,
and I know of no substitute whatever for
the force and beauty of its process.

Henry James, Letter to H. G. Wells

Beauty is in the eye of the beholder.

Margaret Wolfe Hungerford, Molly Bawn

Aesthetic emotion puts man in a state favorable to the
reception of erotic emotion. Art is the accomplice of love.
Take love away and there is no longer art.

Remy de Gourmont, Décadence

Every artist writes his own autobiography.

Havelock Ellis, The New Spirit

Dancing is the loftiest, the most moving, the most beautiful
of the arts, because it is no mere translation or
abstraction from life; it is life itself.

Havelock Ellis, The Dance of Life

Beauty as we feel it is something indescribable:
what it is or what it means can never be said.

George Santayana, The Sense of Beauty

What I like in a good author is not what he says,
but what he whispers.

Logan Pearsall Smith, Afterthoughts

The whole difference between construction and creation is
exactly this: that a thing constructed can only be loved after
it is constructed; but a thing created is loved before it exists.

G. K. Chesterton, Preface to Dickens, Pickwick Papers

Beauty can pierce one like a pain.

Thomas Mann, Buddenbrooks

The artist, like the God of the creation, remains within or
behind or beyond or above his handiwork, invisible, refined
out of existence, indifferent, paring his fingernails.

James Joyce, A Portrait of the Artist as a Young Man

A woman must have money and a room of
her own if she is to write fiction.

Virginia Woolf, A Room of One's Own

Beauty is a mystery. You can neither eat
it nor make flannel out of it.

D. H. Lawrence, Sex Versus Loveliness

The great poet, in writing himself, writes his time.

T. S. Eliot, Shakespeare and the Stoicism of Seneca

Art is unthinkable without risk and spiritual self-sacrifice.

Boris Pasternak, On Modesty and Bravery

I don't know which is more discouraging,
literature or chickens.

E. B. White, Letter to James Thurber

One cannot create an art that speaks to men
when one has nothing to say.

André Malraux, Man's Hope (L'Espoir)

When you reread a classic you do not see more
in the book than you did before; you see
more in you than there was before.

Clifton Fadiman, Any Number Can Play

A musician must make music, an artist must paint, a poet
must write, if he is to be ultimately at peace with
himself. What a man can be, he must be.

Abraham H. Maslow, Motivation and Personality

The key to the mystery of a great artist: that for reasons
unknown to him or to anyone else, he will give away his
energies and his life just to make sure that one note follows
another inevitably. . . . The composer, by doing this, leaves
us at the finish with the feeling that something is right
in the world, that something checks throughout,
something that follows its own laws consistently,
something we can trust, that will never let us down.

Leonard Bernstein, The Joy of Music

The sole substitute for an experience which we have not
ourselves lived through is art and literature.

Alexander Isayevich Solzhenitsyn, Nobel lecture

The true writer has nothing to say. What counts
is the way he says it.

Alain Robbe-Grillet, For a New Novel

The novel is an art form and when you use it for anything
other than art, you pervert it. . . . If you manage to use
it successfully for social, religious, or other purposes,
it is because you make it art first.

Flannery O'Connor, Letter to Father John McCown

Airing one's dirty linen never makes for a masterpiece.

François Truffaut, Bed and Board

One picture is worth a thousand words.

Anonymous

Compassion and Charity

And when ye reap the harvest of your land, thou shalt not
wholly reap the corners of thy field, neither shalt thou
gather the gleanings of thy harvest.
And thou shalt not glean thy vineyard, neither shalt thou
gather every grape of thy vineyard; thou shalt
leave them for the poor and stranger.

The Bible, The Third Book of Moses, Called Leviticus

I was eyes to the blind, and feet was I to the lame.

The Bible, The Book of Job

He that giveth unto the poor shall not lack.

The Bible, The Proverbs

If thou hast abundance, give alms accordingly: if thou have
but a little, be not afraid to give according to that little.

The Bible, The Apocrypha, Tobit

Defraud not the poor of his living, and make
not the needy eyes to wait long.

*The Bible, The Apocrypha, The Wisdom of Jesus
the Son of Sirach, or Ecclesiasticus*

Freely ye have received, freely give.

The Bible, Matthew

Owe no man anything, but to love one another.

The Bible, The Epistle of Paul the Apostle to the Romans

Be swift to hear, slow to speak, slow to wrath.

The Bible, The General Epistle of James

No act of kindness, no matter how small, is ever wasted.

Aesop, The Lion and the Mouse

He plants trees to benefit another generation.

Caecilius Statius, Synephebi. Quoted by Cicero in De Senectute

Charity begins at home.

Terence, Andria

Leave off wishing to deserve any thanks from anyone, or thinking that anyone can ever become grateful.

Gaius Valerius Catullus, Carmina

I have known sorrow and learned to aid the wretched.

Virgil, Aeneid

He doubly benefits the needy who gives quickly.

Publilius Syrus, Maxim

Wealth and children are the adornment of this present life:
but good works, which are lasting, are better in the sight of
thy Lord as to recompense, and better as to hope.

The Koran

Anticipate charity by preventing poverty; assist the reduced
fellowman, either by a considerable gift, or a sum of
money, or by teaching him a trade, or by putting him in the
way of business, so that he may earn an honest livelihood,
and not be forced to the dreadful alternative of holding out
his hand for charity. This is the highest step and the summit
of charity's golden ladder.

Maimonides, Charity's Eight Degrees

Saying is one thing and doing is another.

Michel Eyquem de Montaigne, Essays

In charity there is no excess.

Francis Bacon, Essays

'Tis not enough to help the feeble up,
But to support him after.

William Shakespeare, Timon of Athens

But how shall we expect charity towards others, when we
are uncharitable to ourselves? Charity begins at home, is the
voice of the world; yet is every man his greatest enemy,
and, as it were, his own executioner.

Sir Thomas Browne, Religio Medici

In necessary things, unity; in doubtful things,
liberty; in all things, charity.

Richard Baxter, Motto

In this world, you must be a bit too
kind in order to be kind enough.

Pierre Carlet de Chamblain de Marivaux, Le Jeu de l'Amour et du Hasard

Do as you would be done by, is the surest
method that I know of pleasing.

Philip Dormer Stanhope, Earl of Chesterfield, Letters to His Son

That action is best which procures the greatest
happiness for the greatest numbers.

Francis Hutcheson, Inquiry Concerning Moral Good and Evil

To whom nothing is given, of him can nothing be required.

Henry Fielding, Joseph Andrews

A decent provision for the poor is
the true test of civilization.

Samuel Johnson, From Boswell, Life of Johnson

The heart benevolent and kind
The most resembles God.

Robert Burns, A Winter Night

That best portion of a good man's life,
His little, nameless, unremembered acts
Of kindness and of love.

William Wordsworth, Lines Composed a Few Miles Above Tintern Abbey

The greatest pleasure I know is to do a good action by
stealth, and to have it found out by accident.

Charles Lamb, Table Talk

Be ashamed to die until you have
won some victory for humanity.

Horace Mann, Commencement Address, Antioch College

It is never too late to give up our prejudices.

Henry David Thoreau, Walden

From each according to his abilities,
to each according to his needs.

Karl Marx, Critique of the Gotha Program

Every man feels instinctively that all the beautiful sentiments
in the world weigh less than a single lovely action.

James Russell Lowell, Literary Essays

The worst sin towards our fellow creatures is
not to hate them, but to be indifferent to them:
that's the essence of inhumanity.

George Bernard Shaw, The Devil's Disciple

Let me live in my house by the side of the road
And be a friend to man.

Sam Walter Foss, The House by the Side of the Road

The test of our progress is not whether we add more to the
abundance of those who have much; it is whether we
provide enough for those who have too little.

Franklin Delano Roosevelt, Second Inaugural Address

The greatest disease in the West today is not TB or leprosy;
it is being unwanted, unloved, and uncared for. We can
cure physical diseases with medicine, but the only cure
for loneliness, despair, and hopelessness is love.

Mother Teresa, A Simple Path

And so, my fellow Americans, ask not what your country
can do for you; ask what you can do for your country.
John Fitzgerald Kennedy, Inaugural address

I expect to pass through this world but once; any good
thing therefore that I can do, or any kindness that I can
show to any fellow creature, let me do it now; let me not
defer or neglect it, for I shall not pass this way again.
Anonymous, Proverbial saying

A man of words and not of deeds
Is like a garden full of weeds.
Anonymous, A Man of Words and Not of Deeds

Diligence

Set thine house in order.
The Bible, The Second Book of the Kings

Seest thou a man diligent in his business? He shall stand
before kings.
The Bible, The Proverbs

In her tongue is the law of kindness.
She looketh well to the ways of her household, and eateth
not the bread of idleness.
Her children arise up, and call her blessed.
The Bible, The Proverbs

A little one shall become a thousand,
and a small one a strong nation.
The Bible, The Book of the Prophet Isaiah

Be not ignorant of any thing in a great matter or a small.
*The Bible, The Apocrypha, The Wisdom of Jesus
the Son of Sirach, or Ecclesiasticus*

Consider the lilies of the field, how they grow;
they toil not, neither do they spin.
The Bible, Matthew

Study to be quiet, and to do your own business.
The Bible, The First Epistle of Paul the Apostle to the Thessalonians

Be ye doers of the word, and not hearers only.
The Bible, The General Epistle of James

Badness you can get easily, in quantity: the road is smooth,
and it lies close by. But in front of excellence the immortal
gods have put sweat, and long and steep is the way to it,
and rough at first. But when you come to the top,
then it is easy, even though it is hard.
Hesiod, Works and Days

The gods help them that help themselves.
Aesop, Hercules and the Wagoner

Criticism comes easier than craftsmanship.
Zeuxis, From Pliny the Elder, Natural History

Well begun is half done.
Aristotle, Politics

Practice and thought might gradually forge many an art.

Virgil, Georgics

Practice is the best of all instructors.

Publilius Syrus, Maxim

No thing great is created suddenly, any more than a bunch
of grapes or a fig. If you tell me that you desire a fig,
I answer you that there must be time. Let it first
blossom, then bear fruit, then ripen.

Epictetus, Discourses

He listens well who takes notes.

Dante Alighieri, The Divine Comedy

Iron rusts from disuse; stagnant water loses its purity and
in cold weather becomes frozen; even so does
inaction sap the vigor of the mind.

Leonardo da Vinci, The Notebooks

When the sun shineth, make hay.

John Heywood, Proverbs

Rome was not built in one day.

John Heywood, Proverbs

You're leaping over the hedge before you come to the stile.

Miguel de Cervantes, Don Quixote

Diligence is the mother of good fortune.

Miguel de Cervantes, Don Quixote

By the work one knows the workman.

Jean de La Fontaine, Fables

Whatever is worth doing at all, is worth doing well.

Philip Dormer Stanhope, Earl of Chesterfield, Letters to His Son

Idleness is only the refuge of weak minds.

Philip Dormer Stanhope, Earl of Chesterfield, Letters to His Son

Early to bed and early to rise, makes a man healthy, wealthy, and wise.

Benjamin Franklin, Poor Richard's Almanac

God helps them that help themselves.

Benjamin Franklin, Poor Richard's Almanac

Little strokes,
Fell great oaks.

Benjamin Franklin, Poor Richard's Almanac

If you are idle, be not solitary; if you
are solitary, be not idle.

Samuel Johnson, From Boswell, Life of Johnson

Absence of occupation is not rest,
A mind quite vacant is a mind distress'd.

William Cowper, Retirement

Learning is not attained by chance, it must be sought for
with ardor and attended to with diligence.

Abigail Adams, Letter to John Quincy Adams

Think nothing done while aught remains to do.

Samuel Rogers, Human Life

'Tis a lesson you should heed,
Try, try again.
If at first you don't succeed,
Try, try again.

Thomas H. Palmer, Teacher's Manual

Nothing contributes so much to tranquilize the mind
as a steady purpose — a point on which the
soul may fix its intellectual eye.

Mary Shelley, Frankenstein

The reward of a thing well done, is to have done it.

Ralph Waldo Emerson, Essays

To live without duties is obscene.

Ralph Waldo Emerson, Lectures and Biographical Sketches

The whole secret of the study of nature lies in
learning how to use one's eyes.

George Sand, Nouvelles Lettres d'un Voyageur

And if I should live to be
The last leaf upon the tree
In the spring,
Let them smile, as I do now,
At the old forsaken bough
Where I cling.

Oliver Wendell Holmes, The Last Leaf

Ride on! Rough-shod if need be, smooth-shod
if that will do, but ride on! Ride on over
all obstacles, and win the race!

Charles Dickens, David Copperfield

I know of no more encouraging fact than the
unquestionable ability of man to elevate
his life by a conscious endeavor.
Henry David Thoreau, Walden

Men will lie on their backs, talking about the fall
of man, and never make an effort to get up.
Henry David Thoreau, Life Without Principle

In creating, the only hard thing's to begin;
A grass-blade's no easier to make than an oak.
James Russell Lowell, A Fable for Critics

Do what thy manhood bids thee do,
from none but self expect applause;
He noblest lives and noblest dies who
makes and keeps his self-made laws.
Sir Richard Francis Burton, The Kasîdah of Hâjî Abdû El-Yezdî

There is the greatest practical benefit in making
a few failures early in life.
T. H. Huxley, On Medical Education

Genius is an infinite capacity for taking pains.
Jane Ellice Hopkins, Work Amongst Working Men

Genius is one percent inspiration and
ninety-nine percent perspiration.
Thomas A. Edison, Life

If there's no hatred in a mind
Assault and battery of the wind
Can never tear the linnet from the leaf.
William Butler Yeats, Michael Robartes and the Dancer

I think I can. I think I can. I think I can.
Watty Piper, The Little Engine That Could

The woods are lovely, dark and deep.
But I have promises to keep,
And miles to go before I sleep,
And miles to go before I sleep.
Robert Frost, Stopping by Woods on a Snowy Evening

If only I am keen and hard like the sheer tip of a wedge
Driven by invisible blows,
The rock will split, we shall come at the wonder, we shall
find the Hesperides.
D. H. Lawrence, Song of a Man Who Has Come Through

All this will not be finished in the first one hundred days.
Nor will it be finished in the first one thousand days, nor
in the life of this Administration, nor even perhaps
in our lifetime on this planet. But let us begin.

John Fitzgerald Kennedy, Inaugural address

Keep on truckin'.

R. Crumb, Slogan of cartoon character

The difficult we do immediately. The impossible
takes a little longer.

Anonymous, Slogan of United States Army Service Forces

Faith and Spirituality

Surely the Lord is in this place; and I knew it not.
The Bible, The First Book of Moses, Called Genesis

Man doth not live by bread only, but by every word that
proceedeth out of the mouth of the Lord doth man live.
The Bible, The Fifth Book of Moses, Called Deuteronomy

Canst thou by searching find out God?
The Bible, The Book of Job

The Lord is my shepherd; I shall not want.
He maketh me to lie down in green pastures: he leadeth me
beside the still waters. He restoreth my soul: he leadeth me
in the paths of righteousness for his name's sake. Yea,
though I walk through the valley of the shadow
of death, I will fear no evil: for thou art with me;
thy rod and thy staff they comfort me.
Thou preparest a table before me in the presence
of mine enemies: thou anointest my head with oil;
my cup runneth over.
Surely goodness and mercy shall follow me
all the days of my life: and I will dwell
in the house of the Lord for ever.
The Bible, The Book of Psalms

The grass withereth, the flower fadeth; but the
word of our God shall stand for ever.

The Bible, The Book of the Prophet Isaiah

The kingdom of God is within you.

The Bible, The Gospel According to Saint Luke

He is not a God of the dead, but of the living.

The Bible, The Gospel According to Saint Luke

Blessed are they that have not seen, and yet have believed.

The Bible, The Gospel According to Saint John

All things work together for good to them that love God.

The Bible, The Epistle of Paul the Apostle to the Romans

The fruit of the Spirit is love, joy, peace, long-suffering,
gentleness, goodness, faith, meekness, temperance.

The Bible, The Second Epistle of Paul the Apostle to the Corinthians

Put on the whole armor of God.

The Bible, The Second Epistle of Paul the Apostle to the Corinthians

Faith is the substance of things hoped for,
the evidence of things not seen.

The Bible, The Epistle of Paul the Apostle to the Hebrews

Lead me from the unreal to the real!
Lead me from darkness to light!
Lead me from death to immortality!

The Upanishads, Brihadaranyaka Upanishad

All men have need of the gods.

Homer, Odyssey

Prayer indeed is good, but while calling on the gods a man
should himself lend a hand.

Hippocrates, Regimen

God says: If you come to My House, I will come to yours.

Hillel, From Talmud

Live among men as if God beheld you;
speak to God as if men were listening.

Lucius Annaeus Seneca, Epistles

Is the dwelling place of God anywhere but
in the earth and sea, the air and sky, and
virtue? Why seek we further for deities?

Lucan, The Civil War

When you close your doors, and make darkness within,
remember never to say that you are alone, for you are not
alone; nay, God is within, and your genius is within. And
what need have they of light to see what you are doing?

Epictetus, Discourses

And in His will is our peace.

Dante Alighieri, The Divine Comedy

But Cristes loore and his apostles twelve
He taughte, but first he folwed it hymselve.

Geoffrey Chaucer, The Canterbury Tales

Man proposes, but God disposes.

Thomas à Kempis, Imitation of Christ

I live and love in God's peculiar light.

Michelangelo, Sonnet

A mighty fortress is our God,
A bulwark never failing.
Our helper He amid the flood
Of mortal ills prevailing.

Martin Luther, Ein' Feste Burg

Reason is the greatest enemy that faith has: it never comes
to the aid of spiritual things, but — more frequently than
not — struggles against the divine Word, treating with con-
tempt all that emanates from God.

Martin Luther, Table Talk

Teach us, good Lord, to serve Thee as Thou
deservest:
To give and not to count the cost;
To fight and not to heed the wounds;
To toil and not to seek for rest;
To labor and not ask for any reward
Save that of knowing that we do Thy will.

Saint Ignatius of Loyola, Prayer for Generosity

The nearer to the church, the further from God.

John Heywood, Proverbs

A man with God is always in the majority.

John Knox, Inscription on Reformation Monument, Geneva, Switzerland

What if this present were the world's last night?
John Donne, Holy Sonnets

Persecution is a bad and indirect way to plant religion.
Sir Thomas Browne, Religio Medici

So all we know
Of what they do above
Is that they happy are, and that they love.
Edmund Waller, Upon the Death of My Lady Rich

Men never do evil so completely and cheerfully as when
they do it from religious conviction.
Blaise Pascal, Pensées

We have just religion enough to make us hate, but not
enough to make us love one another.
Jonathan Swift, Thoughts on Various Subjects; from Miscellanies

My country is the world and my religion is to do good.
Thomas Paine, The Rights of Man

Prayer is the soul's sincere desire,
Uttered or unexpressed;
The motion of a hidden fire
That trembles in the breast.
James Montgomery, What Is Prayer?

He prayeth best who loveth best
All things both great and small;
For the dear God who loveth us,
He made and loveth all.
Samuel Taylor Coleridge, The Rime of the Ancient Mariner

Great men are they who see that spiritual is stronger than
any material force, that thoughts rule the world.
Ralph Waldo Emerson, Letters and Social Aims

I would rather believe that God did not exist than believe
that He was indifferent.
George Sand, Impressions et Souvenirs

There lives more faith in honest doubt,
Believe me, than in half the creeds.
Alfred, Lord Tennyson, In Memoriam

You call for faith:
I show you doubt, to prove that faith exists.
The more of doubt, the stronger faith, I say,
If faith o'ercomes doubt.

Robert Browning, Bishop Blougram's Apology

God is seen God
In the star, in the stone, in the flesh,
in the soul and the clod.

Robert Browning, Saul

If it want for faith, thare would be no living
in this world. We couldn't even eat hash
with enny safety, if it want for faith.

Josh Billings, Essays. Faith

Religion . . . is the opium of the people.

Karl Marx, Critique of the Hegelian Philosophy of Right

Whatever a man prays for, he prays for a miracle. Every
prayer reduces itself to this: "Great God, grant
that twice two be not four."

Ivan Sergeyevich Turgenev, Prayer

And almost everyone when age,
Disease, or sorrows strike him,
Inclines to think there is a God,
Or something very like Him.

Arthur Hugh Clough, Dipsychus

Volumes might be written upon the impiety of the pious.

Herbert Spencer, First Principles

If you were to destroy in mankind the belief in immortality,
not only love but every living force maintaining the life of
the world would at once be dried up.

Fëdor Mikhailovich Dostoevski, The Brothers Karamazov

So long as man remains free he strives for nothing so inces-
santly and so painfully as to find someone to worship.

Fëdor Mikhailovich Dostoevski, The Brothers Karamazov

Leave the matter of religion to the family altar, the church,
and the private school, supported entirely by private contri-
butions. Keep the church and the State forever separate.

Ulysses S. Grant, Speech at Des Moines, Iowa

Some keep the Sabbath going to Church —
I keep it, staying at Home —
With a bobolink for a Chorister —
And an Orchard, for a Dome —

Emily Dickinson, No. 324

We, too, have our religion, and it is this:
Help for the living, hope for the dead.

Robert Ingersoll, Address at a child's grave

I don't believe in God because I
don't believe in Mother Goose.

Clarence Darrow, Speech at Toronto

A man must not swallow more beliefs than he can digest.

Havelock Ellis, The Dance of Life

Short arm needs man to reach to Heaven
So ready is Heaven to stoop to him.

Francis Thompson, Grace of the Way

Faith which does not doubt is dead faith.

Miguel de Unamuno, The Agony of Christianity

It is not a carol of joy or glee,
But a prayer that he sends from his heart's deep core . . .
I know why the caged bird sings!

Paul Laurence Dunbar, Sympathy

We have only to believe. And the more threatening and
irreducible reality appears, the more firmly and desperately
must we believe. Then, little by little, we shall see the universal horror unbend, and then smile upon us, and then
take us in its more than human arms.

Pierre Teilhard de Chardin, The Divine Milieu

You pray in your distress and in your need; would that you
might pray also in the fullness of your joy and in your days
of abundance.

Kahlil Gibran, The Prophet

It makes one feel rather good deciding not to be a bitch. . . .
It's sort of what we have instead of God.

Ernest Hemingway, The Sun Also Rises

Have you seen a room from which faith has gone? . . . Like
a marriage from which love has gone. . . . And patience,
patience everywhere like a fog.

Graham Greene, The Potting Shed

Like anybody, I would like to live a long life. Longevity
has its place. But I'm not concerned about that now.
I just want to do God's will. And He's allowed me to
go up to the mountain. And I've looked over, and
I've seen the promised land. I may not get there
with you, but I want you to know tonight that we
as a people will get to the promised land. . . .

Martin Luther King Jr., Address to sanitation workers, Memphis,
Tennessee, the night before his assassination

Everyman, I will go with thee, and be thy guide.

Anonymous, Everyman

God is in the details.

Anonymous, Saying

Fear and Fate

We spend our years as a tale that is told.

The Bible, The Book of Psalms

Be not afraid of sudden fear.

The Bible, The Proverbs

Boast not thyself of tomorrow; for thou knowest
not what a day may bring forth.

The Bible, The Proverbs

The people that walked in darkness have seen a great
light: they that dwell in the land of the shadow
of death, upon them hath the light shined.

The Bible, The Book of the Prophet Isaiah

Rejoice not over thy greatest enemy being dead,
but remember that we die all.

*The Bible, The Apocrypha, The Wisdom of Jesus
the Son of Sirach, or Ecclesiasticus*

He that is today a king tomorrow shall die.

The Bible, The Apocrypha, The Wisdom of Jesus
the Son of Sirach, or Ecclesiasticus

When the dead is at rest, let his remembrance rest; and be comforted for him, when his spirit is departed from him.

The Bible, The Apocrypha, The Wisdom of Jesus
the Son of Sirach, or Ecclesiasticus

A man's character is his fate.

Heraclitus, On the Universe

Death is nothing to us, since when we are, death has not come, and when death has come, we are not.

Epicurus, From Diogenes Laertius, Lives of Eminent Philosophers

For certain is death for the born
And certain is birth for the dead;
Therefore over the inevitable
Thou shouldst not grieve.

Bhagavad Gita

What once sprung from the earth sinks back into the earth.

Lucretius, De Rerum Natura

Why dost thou not retire like a guest sated with the
banquet of life, and with calm mind embrace,
thou fool, a rest that knows no care?

Lucretius, De Rerum Natura

It is easy to go down into Hell; night and day, the gates of
dark Death stand wide; but to climb back again, to retrace
one's steps to the upper air — there's the rub, the task.

Virgil, Aeneid

Pale Death with impartial tread beats at the poor
man's cottage door and at the palaces of kings.

Horace, Odes

Cease to ask what the morrow will bring forth, and set
down as gain each day that Fortune grants.

Horace, Odes

Think not disdainfully of death, but look on it with favor;
for even death is one of the things that Nature wills.

Marcus Aurelius Antoninus, Meditations

What is this world? what asketh men to have?
Now with his love, now in his colde grave
Allone, withouten any compaignye.

Geoffrey Chaucer, The Canterbury Tales

I want death to find me planting my cabbages.

Michel Eyquem de Montaigne, Essays

Live as long as you please, you will strike nothing off the
time you will have to spend dead.

Michel Eyquem de Montaigne, Essays

Fain would I climb, yet fear I to fall.

Sir Walter Ralegh, Written on a windowpane

Sleep after toil, port after stormy seas,
Ease after war, death after life does greatly please.

Edmund Spenser, The Faerie Queene

Nothing is terrible except fear itself.

Francis Bacon, De Augmentis Scientiarum

Of all base passions, fear is most accurs'd.

William Shakespeare, King Henry the Sixth, Part I

True nobility is exempt from fear.

William Shakespeare, King Henry the Sixth, Part II

Extreme fear can neither fight nor fly.

William Shakespeare, The Rape of Lucrece

We cannot hold mortality's strong hand.

William Shakespeare, King John

Be absolute for death.

William Shakespeare, Measure for Measure

Death be not proud, though some have called thee
Mighty and dreadful, for thou art not so,
For those whom thou think'st thou dost overthrow,
Die not, poor death, nor yet canst thou kill me.

John Donne, Holy Sonnets

The good effect of Fortune may be short-lived. To build on
it is to build on sand.

Honorat de Bueil, Marquis de Racan, Poésies Diverses

Who is all-powerful should fear everything.

Pierre Corneille, Cinna

We die only once, and for such a long time!

Molière, Le Dépit Amoureux

They that love beyond the world cannot be separated by it.
Death is but crossing the world, as friends do
the seas; they live in one another still.

William Penn, Some Fruits of Solitude

If a tree dies, plant another in its place.

Linnaeus, From biography by Theodor Magnus Fries

For he counteracts the Devil, who is Death, by brisking
about the life.

Christopher Smart, Jubilate Agno

The earth belongs to the living, not to the dead.

Thomas Jefferson, Letter to John W. Eppes

Death's a debt; his mandamus binds all
alike — no bail, no demurrer.

Richard Brinsley Sheridan, St. Patrick's Day

There's no such thing as chance;
And what to us seems merest accident
Springs from the deepest source of destiny.

Johann Friedrich von Schiller, The Death of Wallenstein

Life is only error,
And death is knowledge.

Johann Friedrich von Schiller, Cassandra

Our hour is marked, and no one can claim a moment
of life beyond what fate has predestined.

Napoleon I, To Dr. Arnott

I want to seize fate by the throat.

Ludwig van Beethoven, Letter to Dr. Franz Wegeler

And come he slow, or come he fast,
It is but Death who comes at last.

Sir Walter Scott, Marmion

'Tis solitude should teach us how to die;
It hath no flatterers; vanity can give
No hollow aid; alone — man with his God must strive.

George Noel Gordon, Lord Byron, Childe Harold's Pilgrimage

Better be killed than frightened to death.

Robert Smith Surtees, Mr. Facey Romford's Hounds

Of all the events which constitute a person's biography,
there is scarcely one . . . to which the world so easily
reconciles itself as to his death.

Nathaniel Hawthorne, The House of the Seven Gables

As for a future life, every man must judge for himself
between conflicting vague probabilities.

*Charles Robert Darwin, From Life and Letters of Charles Darwin,
edited by Francis Darwin*

No life that breathes with human breath
Has ever truly longed for death.

Alfred, Lord Tennyson, The Two Voices

For man is man and master of his fate.

Alfred, Lord Tennyson, Idylls of the King

You never know what life means till you die:
Even throughout life, 'tis death that makes life live,
Gives it whatever the significance.

Robert Browning, The Ring and the Book

Public opinion is a weak tyrant compared with our own
private opinion. What a man thinks of himself, that it is
which determines, or rather, indicates, his fate.

Henry David Thoreau, Walden

There is no good in arguing with the inevitable.
The only argument available with an east
wind is to put on your overcoat.

James Russell Lowell, Democracy

Anyone's death always releases something like an aura of
stupefaction, so difficult is it to grasp this irruption of
nothingness and to believe that it has actually taken place.

Gustave Flaubert, Madame Bovary

A Throw of the Dice Will Never Abolish Chance.

Stéphane Mallarmé, Poésies

Our destiny exercises its influence over us even when, as
yet, we have not learned its nature: it is our
future that lays down the law of our today.

Friedrich Wilhelm Nietzsche, Human, All Too Human

People are always blaming their circumstances for what
they are. I don't believe in circumstances. The people
who get on in this world are the people who get up
and look for the circumstances they want, and,
if they can't find them, make them.

George Bernard Shaw, Mrs. Warren's Profession

Let a man once overcome his selfish terror at his own
finitude, and his finitude is, in one sense, overcome.

George Santayana, The Ethics of Spinoza

Bite on the bullet, old man, and don't
let them think you're afraid.

Rudyard Kipling, The Light That Failed

We should all be concerned about the future because we
will have to spend the rest of our lives there.

Charles F. Kettering, Seed for Thought

I shall never believe that God plays dice with the world.

Albert Einstein, From Philipp Frank, Einstein, His Life and Times

The only thing we have to fear is fear itself.

Franklin Delano Roosevelt, First Inaugural Address

No wreaths please —
especially no hothouse flowers.
Some common memento is better,
something he prized and is known by:
his old clothes — a few books perhaps.

William Carlos Williams, Tract

Birth, and copulation, and death.
That's all the facts when you come to brass tacks.

T. S. Eliot, Sweeney Agonistes

What the dead had no speech for, when living,
They can tell you, being dead: the communication
Of the dead is tongued with fire beyond the language of
the living.

T. S. Eliot, Four Quartets

Tell us your phobias and we will tell you what you are
afraid of.

Robert Benchley, Phobias

The cradle rocks above an abyss, and common sense
tells us that our existence is but a brief crack of
light between two eternities of darkness.

Vladimir Nabokov, Speak, Memory

Life is its own journey, presupposes its own
change and movement, and one tries to
arrest them at one's eternal peril.

Laurens Van der Post, Venture to the Interior

I shall tell you a great secret, my friend. Do not wait for the
last judgment. It takes place every day.

Albert Camus, The Fall

Linus: After you've died, do you get to come back?
Charlie Brown: If they stamp your hand.

Charles M. Schulz, Peanuts

It's not that I'm afraid to die. I just don't
want to be there when it happens.

Woody Allen, Without Feathers

Friendship

He that repeateth a matter separateth very
friends.

The Bible, The Proverbs

A man that hath friends must show himself friendly: and
there is a friend that sticketh closer than a brother.

The Bible, The Proverbs

As cold waters to a thirsty soul, so is
good news from a far country.

The Bible, The Proverbs

Better is a neighbor that is near than a brother far off.

The Bible, The Proverbs

A faithful friend is the medicine of life.

*The Bible, The Apocrypha, The Wisdom of Jesus
the Son of Sirach, or Ecclesiasticus*

Forsake not an old friend; for the new is not
comparable to him: a new friend is as new wine;
when it is old, thou shalt drink it with pleasure.

The Bible, The Apocrypha, The Wisdom of Jesus
the Son of Sirach, or Ecclesiasticus

We secure our friends not by accepting
favors but by doing them.

Thucydides, Peloponnesian War

What is a friend? A single soul dwelling in two bodies.

Aristotle, From Diogenes Laertius, Lives of Eminent Philosophers

Verily great grace may go
With a little gift; and precious are all
things that come from friends.

Theocritus, Idylls

Nothing is there more friendly to
a man than a friend in need.

Titus Maccius Plautus, Epidicus

Who sees Me in all,
And sees all in Me,
For him I am not lost,
And he is not lost for Me.

Bhagavad Gita

The shifts of Fortune test the reliability of friends.

Marcus Tullius Cicero, De Amicitia

A friend is, as it were, a second self.

Marcus Tullius Cicero, De Amicitia

Prosperity makes friends, adversity tries them.

Publilius Syrus, Maxim

He who loves me, let him follow me.

Philip VI, Attributed

My sone, keep wel thy tonge, and keep thy freend.

Geoffrey Chaucer, The Canterbury Tales

Two heads are better than one.

John Heywood, Proverbs

But in deed,
A friend is never known till a man have need.

John Heywood, Proverbs

The more the merrier.

John Heywood, Proverbs

If you press me to say why I loved him, I can say no more
than it was because he was he and I was I.

Michel Eyquem de Montaigne, Essays

Small cheer and great welcome makes a merry feast.

William Shakespeare, The Comedy of Errors

I count myself in nothing else so happy
As in a soul remembering my good friends.

William Shakespeare, King Richard the Second

Better a little chiding than a great deal of heartbreak.

William Shakespeare, The Merry Wives of Windsor

A friend should bear his friend's infirmities.

William Shakespeare, Julius Caesar

But if the while I think on thee, dear friend,
All losses are restor'd and sorrows end.

William Shakespeare, Sonnet 30

To me, fair friend, you never can be old,
For as you were when first your eye I ey'd,
Such seems your beauty still.

William Shakespeare, Sonnet 104

Every one that flatters thee
Is no friend in misery.
Words are easy, like the wind;
Faithful friends are hard to find.
Every man will be thy friend
Whilst thou hast wherewith to spend;
But if store of crowns be scant,
No man will supply thy want.
Richard Barnfield, Poems: In Divers Humours

Old friends are best. King James used to call for his
old shoes; they were easiest for his feet.
John Selden, Table Talk

No man is born unto himself alone;
Who lives unto himself, he lives to none.
Francis Quarles, Esther

The more we love our friends, the less we flatter them; it is
by excusing nothing that pure love shows itself.
Molière, Le Misanthrope

It is a wonderful seasoning of all enjoyments
to think of those we love.
Molière, Le Misanthrope

True friendship is never serene.

Marie de Rabutin-Chantal, Marquise de Sévigné, Lettres

From wine what sudden friendship springs!

John Gay, Fables

If a man does not make new acquaintances as he advances
through life, he will soon find himself left alone. A man,
sir, should keep his friendship in a constant repair.

Samuel Johnson, From James Boswell, Life of Johnson

To let friendship die away by negligence and silence, is
certainly not wise. It is voluntarily to throw away one
of the greatest comforts of this weary pilgrimage.

Samuel Johnson, From Boswell, Life of Johnson

I look upon every day to be lost, in which I
do not make a new acquaintance.

Samuel Johnson, From Boswell, Life of Johnson

We cannot tell the precise moment when friendship is
formed. As in filling a vessel drop by drop, there is at last a
drop which makes it run over; so in a series of kindnesses
there is at last one which makes the heart run over.

James Boswell, Life of Johnson

To know of someone here and there whom we accord
with, who is living on with us, even in silence —
this makes our earthly ball a peopled garden.

Johann Wolfgang von Goethe, Wilhelm Meister's Apprenticeship

I was angry with my friend;
I told my wrath, my wrath did end.
I was angry with my foe;
I told it not, my wrath did grow.

William Blake, Songs of Experience

Flowers are lovely; love is flower-like;
Friendship is a sheltering tree.

Samuel Taylor Coleridge, Youth and Age

"Friendship is Love without his wings!"

George Noel Gordon, Lord Byron, L'Amitié Est l'Amour sans Ailes

A friend may well be reckoned the masterpiece of Nature.

Ralph Waldo Emerson, Essays

The only reward of virtue is virtue; the only
way to have a friend is to be one.

Ralph Waldo Emerson, Essays

I do then with my friends as I do with my books. I would
have them where I can find them, but I seldom use them.
Ralph Waldo Emerson, Essays

He makes no friend who never made a foe.
Alfred, Lord Tennyson, Idylls of the King

A friend in power is a friend lost.
Henry Adams, The Education of Henry Adams

So long as we love we serve; so long as we are loved by
others, I would almost say that we are indispensable; and
no man is useless while he has a friend.
Robert Louis Stevenson, Across the Plains

Think where man's glory most begins and ends,
And say my glory was I had such friends.
William Butler Yeats, Last Poems

Only solitary men know the full joys of friendship.
Others have their family; but to a solitary and
an exile his friends are everything.
Willa Cather, Shadows on the Rock

If I had to choose between betraying my country
and betraying my friend, I hope I should
have the guts to betray my country.

E. M. Forster, Two Cheers for Democracy

None of the new spiders ever quite took her place in his
heart. She was in a class by herself. It is not often
that someone comes along who is a true friend
and a good writer. Charlotte was both.

E. B. White, Charlotte's Web

People, people who need people
Are the luckiest people in the world.

Bob Merrill, People

Oh I get by with a little help from my friends
Mmm get high with a little help from my friends.

John Lennon and Sir Paul McCartney, With a Little Help from My Friends

Fulfillment and Happiness

Be cheerful while you are alive.
Ptahhotpe, The Maxims of Ptahhotpe

A merry heart doeth good like a medicine.
The Bible, The Proverbs

Better is a handful with quietness, than both the
hands full with travail and vexation of spirit.
The Bible, Ecclesiastes; or, The Preacher

A man hath no better thing under the sun, than to eat,
and to drink, and to be merry.
The Bible, Ecclesiastes; or, The Preacher

Let thy life be sincere.
*The Bible, The Apocrypha, The Wisdom of Jesus
the Son of Sirach, or Ecclesiasticus*

Gladness of the heart is the life of a man, and the
joyfulness of a man prolongeth his days.
*The Bible, The Apocrypha, The Wisdom of Jesus
the Son of Sirach, or Ecclesiasticus*

Ask, and it shall be given you; seek, and ye shall find;
knock, and it shall be opened unto you.

The Bible, Matthew

Manifest plainness,
Embrace simplicity,
Reduce selfishness,
Have few desires.

Lao-tzu, The Way of Lao-tzu

To yield is to be preserved whole.
To be bent is to become straight.
To be empty is to be full.
To be worn out is to be renewed.
To have little is to possess.
To have plenty is to be perplexed.

Lao-tzu, The Way of Lao-tzu

Having the fewest wants, I am nearest to the gods.

Socrates, From Diogenes Laertius, Lives of Eminent Philosophers

The life which is unexamined is not worth living.

Plato, Apology

It is impossible to live pleasurably without living wisely,
well, and justly, and impossible to live wisely,
well, and justly without living pleasurably.

Epicurus, From Diogenes Laertius, Lives of Eminent Philosophers

Let us go singing as far as we go:
the road will be less tedious.

Virgil, Eclogues

We rarely find anyone who can say he has lived a happy
life, and who, content with his life, can retire from the
world like a satisfied guest.

Horace, Satires

No man is happy who does not think himself so.

Publilius Syrus, Maxim

Mark how fleeting and paltry is the estate of man —
yesterday in embryo, tomorrow a mummy or ashes. So for
the hairsbreadth of time assigned to thee, live rationally,
and part with life cheerfully, as drops the ripe olive,
extolling the season that bore it and the tree that matured it.

Marcus Aurelius Antoninus, Meditations

Very little is needed to make a happy life.

Marcus Aurelius Antoninus, Meditations

To laugh is proper to man.

François Rabelais, Gargantua and Pantagruel

Enough is as good as a feast.

John Heywood, Proverbs

'Tis better to be lowly born,
And range with humble livers in content,
Than to be perk'd up in a glist'ring grief
And wear a golden sorrow.

William Shakespeare, King Henry the Eighth

Let all thy joys be as the month of May,
And all thy days be as a marriage day:
Let sorrow, sickness, and a troubled mind
Be stranger to thee.

Francis Quarles, To a Bride

Nor love thy life, nor hate; but what thou liv'st
Live well; how long or short permit to Heaven.

John Milton, Paradise Lost

Variety is the soul of pleasure.

Aphra Behn, The Rover

May you live all the days of your life.
Jonathan Swift, Polite Conversation

True happiness is of a retired nature, and an enemy to
pomp and noise; it arises, in the first place, from the enjoyment of one's self; and, in the next, from the friendship and
conversation of a few select companions.
Joseph Addison, The Spectator

[Optimism] is a mania for saying things
are well when one is in hell.
Voltaire, Candide

Avarice and happiness never saw each other, how then
should they become acquainted.
Benjamin Franklin, Poor Richard's Almanac

Human felicity is produced not so much by great pieces of
good fortune that seldom happen, as by little advantages
that occur every day.
Benjamin Franklin, Autobiography

Morality is not properly the doctrine of how we may make
ourselves happy, but how we may make
ourselves worthy of happiness.
Immanuel Kant, Critique of Practical Reason

The most wasted day of all is that on
which we have not laughed.

Sébastien Roch Nicolas Chamfort, Maxims and Thoughts

The greatest happiness for the thinking man is to have
fathomed the fathomable, and to quietly
revere the unfathomable.

Johann Wolfgang von Goethe, Proverbs in Prose

Who does not love wine, women, and song
Remains a fool his whole life long.

Johann Heinrich Voss, Attributed

You never know what is enough unless you
know what is more than enough.

William Blake, The Marriage of Heaven and Hell

But pleasures are like poppies spread —
You seize the flow'r, its bloom is shed;
Or like the snow falls in the river —
A moment white — then melts forever.

Robert Burns, Tam o' Shanter

Pain is short, and joy is eternal.

Johann Friedrich von Schiller, The Maid of Orleans

Never give way to melancholy; resist it steadily,
for the habit will encroach.

Sydney Smith, Lady Holland's Memoir

We know nothing of tomorrow; our business
is to be good and happy today.

Sydney Smith, Lady Holland's Memoir

Even in the common affairs of life, in love, friendship,
and marriage, how little security have we when we
trust our happiness in the hands of others!

William Hazlitt, Table Talk

The supreme happiness of life is the
conviction that we are loved.

Victor Hugo, Les Misérables

Crossing a bare common, in snow puddles, at twilight,
under a clouded sky, without having in my thoughts any
occurrence of special good fortune, I have enjoyed a
perfect exhilaration. I am glad to the brink of fear.

Ralph Waldo Emerson, Nature

Nothing can bring you peace but yourself.

Ralph Waldo Emerson, Essays

Nothing great was ever achieved without enthusiasm.
Ralph Waldo Emerson, Essays

Variety is the mother of Enjoyment.
Benjamin Disraeli, Earl of Beaconsfield, Vivian Grey

Life in common among people who love
each other is the ideal of happiness.
George Sand, Histoire de Ma Vie

Ask yourself whether you are happy,
and you cease to be so.
John Stuart Mill, Autobiography

To own a bit of ground, to scratch it with a hoe,
to plant seeds, and watch the renewal of life — this
is the commonest delight of the race, the
most satisfactory thing a man can do.
Charles Dudley Warner, My Summer in a Garden

Live all you can; it's a mistake not to. It doesn't so
much matter what you do in particular, so long as you
have your life. If you haven't had that what have you
had? . . . What one loses one loses; make no mistake
about that. . . . The right time is any time that
one is still so lucky as to have. . . . Live!
Henry James, The Ambassadors

There is no duty we so much underrate
as the duty of being happy.

Robert Louis Stevenson, Virginibus Puerisque

In this world there are only two tragedies. One is not getting what one wants, and the other is getting it.

Oscar Wilde, Lady Windermere's Fan

We have no more right to consume happiness without producing it than to consume wealth without producing it.

George Bernard Shaw, Candida

Let your boat of life be light, packed with only what you
need — a homely home and simple pleasures, one or
two friends, worth the name, someone to love and
someone to love you, a cat, a dog, and a pipe
or two, enough to eat and enough to wear,
and a little more than enough to drink;
for thirst is a dangerous thing.

Jerome K. Jerome, Three Men in a Boat

Happiness is the only sanction of life; where happiness
fails, existence remains a mad and lamentable experiment.

George Santayana, The Life of Reason

There are two things to aim at in life: first, to get what you want; and, after that, to enjoy it. Only the wisest of mankind achieve the second.

Logan Pearsall Smith, Afterthoughts

That is happiness; to be dissolved into something complete and great.

Willa Cather, My Ántonia

How simple and frugal a thing is happiness: a glass of wine, a roast chestnut, a wretched little brazier, the sound of the sea. . . . All that is required to feel that here and now is happiness is a simple, frugal heart.

Nikos Kazantzakis, Zorba the Greek

For man, as for flower and beast and bird, the supreme triumph is to be most vividly, most perfectly alive.

D. H. Lawrence, Apocalypse

There is only one success — to be able to spend your life in your own way.

Christopher Morley, Where the Blue Begins

It's good to be just plain happy; it's a little better to
know that you're happy; but to understand that you're
happy and to know why and how . . . and still be happy,
be happy in the being and the knowing, well
that is beyond happiness, that is bliss.

Henry Miller, The Colossus of Maroussi

No human being can really understand another,
and no one can arrange another's happiness.

Graham Greene, The Heart of the Matter

My unhappiness was the unhappiness of
a person who could not say no.

Dazai Osamu, No Longer Human

Fear tastes like a rusty knife and do not let her into
your house. Courage tastes of blood. Stand up
straight. Admire the world. Relish the love
of a gentle woman. Trust in the Lord.

John Cheever, The Wapshot Chronicle

Guided by my heritage of a love of beauty and a
respect for strength — in search of my
mother's garden, I found my own.

Alice Walker, In Search of Our Mothers' Gardens

Health

There is no riches above a sound body.

The Bible, The Apocrypha, The Wisdom of Jesus
the Son of Sirach, or Ecclesiasticus

Words are the physicians of a mind diseased.

Aeschylus, Prometheus Bound

Healing is a matter of time, but it is
sometimes also a matter of opportunity.

Hippocrates, Precepts

A wise man should consider that health is the greatest of
human blessings, and learn how by his own
thought to derive benefit from his illnesses.

Hippocrates, Regimen in Health

You should pray for a sound mind in a sound body.

Juvenal, Satires

It is unseasonable and unwholesome in all months that
have not an r in their name to eat an oyster.

William Butler, Dyet's Dry Dinner

Go to bed with the lamb, and rise with the lark.

John Lyly, Euphues and His England

There is a wisdom in this beyond the rules of physic. A man's own observation, what he finds good of and what he finds hurt of, is the best physic to preserve health.

Francis Bacon, Essays

Unquiet meals make ill digestions.

William Shakespeare, The Comedy of Errors

As a surfeit of the sweetest things
The deepest loathing to the stomach brings.

William Shakespeare, A Midsummer-Night's Dream

Eat no onions nor garlic, for we are to utter sweet breath.

William Shakespeare, A Midsummer-Night's Dream

Though I look old, yet I am strong and lusty;
For in my youth I never did apply
Hot and rebellious liquors in my blood.

William Shakespeare, As You Like It

Drink not the third glass, which thou canst not tame
When once it is within thee.

George Herbert, The Temple

'Tis not the meat, but 'tis the appetite
Makes eating a delight.
Sir John Suckling, Fragmenta Aurea

One must eat to live, and not live to eat.
Molière, Amphitryon

A man is as old as his arteries.
*Thomas Sydenham, Quoted in Bulletin of
the New York Academy of Medicine*

Better to hunt in fields, for health unbought,
Than fee the doctor for a nauseous draught.
The wise, for cure, on exercise depend;
God never made his work for man to mend.
John Dryden, Epistle to John Driden of Chesterton

Eat not to dullness; drink not to elevation.
Benjamin Franklin, Autobiography

Think in the morning. Act in the noon.
Eat in the evening. Sleep in the night.
William Blake, The Marriage of Heaven and Hell

Give me health and a day, and I will make
the pomp of emperors ridiculous.
Ralph Waldo Emerson, Nature

Health that mocks the doctor's rules,
Knowledge never learned of schools.
John Greenleaf Whittier, The Barefoot Boy

If I'd known I was going to live this long,
I'd have taken better care of myself.
Eubie Blake, Attributed

You can no more keep a martini in the refrigerator than you
can keep a kiss there. The proper union of gin and
vermouth is a great and sudden glory; it is one of the
happiest marriages on earth and one of the shortest-lived.
Bernard De Voto, The Hour

Obesity is a mental state, a disease brought
on by boredom and disappointment.
Cyril Connolly, The Unquiet Grave

An apple a day keeps the doctor away.
Anonymous, Current since the nineteenth century

Honor

Before honor is humility.

The Bible, The Proverbs

A good name is rather to be chosen than great riches.

The Bible, The Proverbs

A man's pride shall bring him low: but honor shall uphold
the humble in spirit.

The Bible, The Proverbs

Be not as a lion in thy house, nor frantic among thy servants.
Let not thine hand be stretched out to receive,
and shut when thou shouldest repay.

*The Bible, The Apocrypha, The Wisdom of Jesus
the Son of Sirach, or Ecclesiasticus*

Leave not a stain in thine honor.

*The Bible, The Apocrypha, The Wisdom of Jesus
the Son of Sirach, or Ecclesiasticus*

Of men who have a sense of honor, more come
through alive than are slain, but from those who
flee comes neither glory nor any help.

Homer, Iliad

All men have in themselves that which is truly
honorable. Only they do not think of it.

Mencius, Works

There is no witness so dreadful, no accuser so terrible as
the conscience that dwells in the heart of every man.

Polybius, History

If a man aspires to the highest place, it is no dishonor to
him to halt at the second, or even at the third.

Marcus Tullius Cicero, Orator

As long as rivers shall run down to the sea,
or shadows touch the mountain slopes, or stars graze
in the vault of heaven, so long shall your honor,
your name, your praises endure.

Virgil, Aeneid

A good reputation is more valuable than money.

Publilius Syrus, Maxim

Men do not care how nobly they live, but only how long,
although it is within the reach of every man to live
nobly, but within no man's power to live long.

Lucius Annaeus Seneca, Epistles

Never esteem anything as of advantage to you that will
make you break your word or lose your self-respect.

Marcus Aurelius Antoninus, Meditations

Walk not on the earth exultantly, for thou canst
not cleave the earth, neither shalt thou reach
to the mountains in height.

The Koran

Worldly renown is naught but a breath of wind, which
now comes this way and now comes that, and
changes name because it changes quarter.

Dante Alighieri, The Divine Comedy

Reputation is an idle and most false imposition; oft
got without merit, and lost without deserving.

William Shakespeare, Othello

It makes us, or it mars us.

William Shakespeare, Othello

Honor is like an island, rugged and without a beach;
once we have left it, we can never return.

Nicolas Boileau-Despréaux, Satire

No man was ever written out of reputation but by himself.

Richard Bentley, From J. H. Monk, Life of Bentley

A wit's a feather, and a chief a rod;
An honest man's the noblest work of God.

Alexander Pope, An Essay on Man

Our hoard is little, but our hearts are great.

Alfred, Lord Tennyson, Idylls of the King

I say to you in all sadness of conviction, that to think great
thoughts you must be heroes as well as idealists.

Oliver Wendell Holmes Jr., The Profession of the Law

This old anvil laughs at many broken hammers.
There are men who can't be bought.

Carl Sandburg, The People Will Live On

The difference between a moral man and a man of honor is
that the latter regrets a discreditable act, even when it has
worked and he has not been caught.

H. L. Mencken, Prejudices

There could be no honor in a sure success, but
much might be wrested from a sure defeat.

T. E. Lawrence, Revolt in the Desert

For every man who lives without freedom,
the rest of us must face the guilt.

Lillian Hellman, Watch on the Rhine

Hope

Weeping may endure for a night,
but joy cometh in the morning.

The Bible, The Book of Psalms

Hope deferred maketh the heart sick.

The Bible, The Proverbs

Hope is a waking dream.

Aristotle, From Diogenes Laertius, Lives of Eminent Philosophers

A likely impossibility is always preferable
to an unconvincing possibility.

Aristotle, Poetics

No one regards what is before his feet;
we all gaze at the stars.

Quintus Ennius, Iphigenia. From Cicero, De Divinatione

While there's life, there's hope.

Terence, Heauton Timoroumenos

Without hope we live in desire.
Dante Alighieri, The Divine Comedy

It behoved that there should be sin; but all shall be well,
and all shall be well, and all manner of thing shall be well.
Juliana of Norwich, Revelations of Divine Love

For I have seyn, of a ful misty morwe
Folowen ful often a myrie someris day.
Geoffrey Chaucer, Troilus and Criseyde

Hope is a good breakfast, but it is a bad supper.
Francis Bacon, Apothegms

It is always darkest just before the day dawneth.
Thomas Fuller, Pisgah Sight

Fear cannot be without hope nor hope without fear.
Benedict Spinoza, Ethics

Hope springs eternal in the human breast:
Man never is, but always to be blest.
Alexander Pope, An Essay on Man

He that lives upon hope will die fasting.
Benjamin Franklin, Poor Richard's Almanac

Hope, like the gleaming taper's light,
Adorns and cheers our way;
And still, as darker grows the night,
Emits a brighter ray.
Oliver Goldsmith, The Captivity, An Oratorio

There is another and a better world.
August Friedrich Ferdinand von Kotzebue, The Stranger

Work without Hope draws nectar in a sieve,
And Hope without an object cannot live.
Samuel Taylor Coleridge, Work Without Hope

The surest way to get a thing in this life is to be prepared
for doing without it, to the exclusion even of hope.
Jane Welsh Carlyle, Journal

The strongest and sweetest songs yet remain to be sung.
Walt Whitman, November Boughs

"Hope" is the thing with feathers —
That perches in the soul —
And sings the tune without the words —
And never stops — at all —
Emily Dickinson, No. 254

There is nothing so well known as that we should
not expect something for nothing — but we
all do and call it Hope.
Edgar Watson Howe, Country Town Sayings

We are all in the gutter, but some
of us are looking at the stars.
Oscar Wilde, Lady Windermere's Fan

There is in most Americans some spark of idealism,
which can be fanned into a flame. It takes sometimes
a divining rod to find what it is; but when found, and
that means often, when disclosed to the owners,
the results are often most extraordinary.
Louis D. Brandeis, The Words of Justice Brandeis

You see things; and you say, "Why?" But I dream things
that never were; and I say, "Why not?"
George Bernard Shaw, Back to Methuselah

In dreams begins responsibility.

William Butler Yeats, Responsibilities

Believe in life! Always human beings will live and
progress to greater, broader, and fuller life.

William Edward Burghardt Du Bois, Last message to the world

A graveyard of buried hopes is about as
romantic a thing as one can imagine.

L. M. Montgomery, Anne of Green Gables

'Twixt the optimist and pessimist
The difference is droll:
The optimist sees the doughnut
But the pessimist sees the hole.

McLandburgh Wilson, Optimist and Pessimist

So always look for the silver lining
And try to find the sunny side of life.

P. G. Wodehouse, Sally

To dream the impossible dream,
To reach the unreachable star!

Joe Darion, The Impossible Dream

Human Nature

Go not empty unto thy mother in law.
The Bible, The Book of Ruth

Wrath killeth the foolish man, and
envy slayeth the silly one.
The Bible, The Book of Job

Pride goeth before destruction, and an
haughty spirit before a fall.
The Bible, The Proverbs

A fool's mouth is his destruction.
The Bible, The Proverbs

Train up a child in the way he should go; and when
he is old, he will not depart from it.
The Bible, The Proverbs

Hide thyself as it were for a little moment,
until the indignation be overpast.
The Bible, The Book of the Prophet Isaiah

Now therefore keep thy sorrow to thyself, and bear with a
good courage that which hath befallen thee.

The Bible, The Apocrypha, II Esdras

Be not curious in unnecessary matters: for more things
are showed unto thee than men understand.

The Bible, The Apocrypha, The Wisdom of Jesus the Son of Sirach, or Ecclesiasticus

So is a word better than a gift.

*The Bible, The Apocrypha, The Wisdom of Jesus
the Son of Sirach, or Ecclesiasticus*

Be not made a beggar by banqueting upon borrowing.

*The Bible, The Apocrypha, The Wisdom of Jesus
the Son of Sirach, or Ecclesiasticus*

Whether it be to friend or foe, talk not of other men's lives.

*The Bible, The Apocrypha, The Wisdom of Jesus
the Son of Sirach, or Ecclesiasticus*

A man's attire, and excessive laughter,
and gait, show what he is.

*The Bible, The Apocrypha, The Wisdom of Jesus
the Son of Sirach, or Ecclesiasticus*

Let thy speech be short, comprehending
much in few words.

*The Bible, The Apocrypha, The Wisdom of Jesus
the Son of Sirach, or Ecclesiasticus*

No man can serve two masters: for either he will hate the
one, and love the other; or else he will hold to the one, and
despise the other. Ye cannot serve God and mammon.

The Bible, Matthew

Not that which goeth into the mouth defileth a man; but
that which cometh out of the mouth, this defileth a man.

The Bible, Matthew

Many that are first shall be last; and the last shall be first.

The Bible, Matthew

If a house be divided against itself, that house cannot stand.

The Bible, The Gospel According to Saint Mark

A crust eaten in peace is better than a
banquet partaken in anxiety.

Aesop, The Town Mouse and the Country Mouse

By nature, men are nearly alike; by practice,
they get to be wide apart.

Confucius, Analects

Nobody likes the man who brings bad news.

Sophocles, Antigone

You cannot teach a crab to walk straight.

Aristophanes, Peace

Of all the animals, the boy is the most unmanageable.

Plato, Laws

The ape, vilest of beasts, how like to us.

Quintus Ennius, From Cicero, De Natura Deorum

Never less idle than when wholly idle, nor less
alone than when wholly alone.

Marcus Tullius Cicero, De Officiis

In Rome you long for the country; in the country — oh
inconstant! — you praise the distant city to the stars.

Horace, Satires

You can tell the character of every man when
you see how he receives praise.

Lucius Annaeus Seneca, Epistles

There is no great genius without some touch of madness.

Lucius Annaeus Seneca, Moral Essays

Man is the only one that knows nothing, that can learn
nothing without being taught. He can neither speak
nor walk nor eat, and in short he can do nothing
at the prompting of nature only, but weep.

Pliny the Elder, Natural History

Remember that you ought to behave in life as you would at
a banquet. As something is being passed around it comes
to you; stretch out your hand, take a portion of it politely.
It passes on; do not detain it. Or it has not come to you
yet; do not project your desire to meet it, but wait
until it comes in front of you. So act toward children,
so toward a wife, so toward office, so toward wealth.

Epictetus, The Encheiridion

Early impressions are hard to eradicate from the mind.
When once wool has been dyed purple, who can
restore it to its previous whiteness?

Saint Jerome, Letter

A fair request should be followed by the deed in silence.

Dante Alighieri, The Divine Comedy

Manners maketh man.

William of Wykeham, Motto

Ech man for hymself.

Geoffrey Chaucer, The Canterbury Tales

What thyng we may nat lightly have,
Thereafter wol we crie al day and crave.

Geoffrey Chaucer, The Canterbury Tales

And when he is out of sight, quickly
also is he out of mind.

Thomas à Kempis, Imitation of Christ

Comparisons are odious.

John Fortescue, De Laudibus Legum Angliae

The world wants to be deceived.

Sebastian Brant, The Ship of Fools

When neither their property nor their honor is touched,
the majority of men live content.

Niccolò Machiavelli, The Prince

Whoever desires to found a state and give it laws,
must start with assuming that all men are bad
and ever ready to display their vicious nature,
whenever they may find occasion for it.

Niccolò Machiavelli, Discourse upon the First Ten Books of Livy

Haste maketh waste.

John Heywood, Proverbs

Look ere ye leap.

John Heywood, Proverbs

Children learn to creep ere they can learn to go.

John Heywood, Proverbs

Burnt child fire dreadeth.

John Heywood, Proverbs

The souls of emperors and cobblers are cast in the same
mold. . . . The same reason that makes us bicker with
a neighbor creates a war between princes.

Michel Eyquem de Montaigne, Essays

A man must be a little mad if he does
not want to be even more stupid.

Michel Eyquem de Montaigne, Essays

Wisely and slow; they stumble that run fast.

William Shakespeare, Romeo and Juliet

It is a wise father that knows his own child.

William Shakespeare, The Merchant of Venice

Men of few words are the best men.

William Shakespeare, King Henry the Fifth

Suit the action to the word, the word to the action;
with this special observance, that you
o'erstep not the modesty of nature.

William Shakespeare, Hamlet

He that is proud eats up himself; pride is his own glass,
his own trumpet, his own chronicle.

William Shakespeare, Troilus and Cressida

The art of our necessities is strange,
That can make vile things precious.

William Shakespeare, King Lear

Press not a falling man too far.
William Shakespeare, King Henry the Eighth

No man is an island, entire of itself; every man is a
piece of the continent, a part of the main.
John Donne, Devotions upon Emergent Occasions

As no man is born an artist, so no man is born an angler.
Izaak Walton, The Compleat Angler

I love such mirth as does not make friends ashamed
to look upon one another next morning.
Izaak Walton, The Compleat Angler

It is impossible to please all the world and one's father.
Jean de La Fontaine, Fables

Those whose conduct gives room for talk are always the
first to attack their neighbors.
Molière, Tartuffe

I have discovered that all human evil comes from this,
man's being unable to sit still in a room.
Blaise Pascal, Pensées

Blood is thicker than water.

John Ray, English Proverbs

New opinions are always suspected, and usually
opposed, without any other reason but because
they are not already common.

John Locke, Essay Concerning Human Understanding

Mankind, by the perverse depravity of their nature, esteem
that which they have most desired as of no value the
moment it is possessed, and torment themselves with
fruitless wishes for that which is beyond their reach.

François de Salignac de la Mothe Fénelon, Télémaque

When you fall into a man's conversation, the first thing you
should consider is, whether he has a greater inclination
to hear you, or that you should hear him.

Sir Richard Steele, The Spectator

To err is human, to forgive divine.

Alexander Pope, An Essay on Criticism

Not always actions show the man: we find
Who does a kindness is not therefore kind.

Alexander Pope, Moral Essays

An injury is much sooner forgotten than an insult.
Philip Dormer Stanhope, Earl of Chesterfield, Letters to His Son

The secret of being a bore is to tell everything.
Voltaire, Sept Discours en Vers sur l'Homme

After three days men grow weary, of a wench,
a guest, and weather rainy.
Benjamin Franklin, Poor Richard's Almanac

Three may keep a secret, if two of them are dead.
Benjamin Franklin, Poor Richard's Almanac

Of all the griefs that harass the distrest,
Sure the most bitter is a scornful jest.
Samuel Johnson, London

Curiosity is one of the permanent and certain
characteristics of a vigorous mind.
Samuel Johnson, The Rambler

From fanaticism to barbarism is only one step.
Denis Diderot, Essai sur le Mérite de la Vertu

Out of wood so crooked and perverse as that which man is
made of, nothing absolutely straight can ever be wrought.
Immanuel Kant, The Idea of a Universal History

People are not always what they seem.
Gotthold Ephraim Lessing, Nathan der Weise

Say not you know another entirely, till you
have divided an inheritance with him.
Johann Kaspar Lavater, Aphorisms on Man

We can't form our children on our own concepts; we must
take them and love them as God gives them to us.
Johann Wolfgang von Goethe, Hermann and Dorothea

Just trust yourself, then you will know how to live.
Johann Wolfgang von Goethe, Faust

A man's manners are a mirror in
which he shows his portrait.
Johann Wolfgang von Goethe, Proverbs in Prose

Women sometimes forgive a man who forces the
opportunity, but never a man who misses one.
Charles Maurice de Talleyrand-Périgord, Attributed

Punctuality is the politeness of kings.

Louis XVIII, A favorite saying

Can I see another's woe,
And not be in sorrow too?
Can I see another's grief,
And not seek for kind relief?

William Blake, Songs of Innocence

The social, friendly, honest man,
Whate'er he be,
'Tis he fulfills great Nature's plan,
And none but he!

Robert Burns, Second Epistle to J. Lapraik

If you want to know yourself,
Just look how others do it;
If you want to understand others,
Look into your own heart.

Johann Friedrich von Schiller, Tabulae Votivae

Pleasure's a sin, and sometimes sin's a pleasure.

George Noel Gordon, Lord Byron, Don Juan

Even good men like to make the public stare.

George Noel Gordon, Lord Byron, Don Juan

No man who has once heartily and wholly laughed
can be altogether irreclaimably bad.

Thomas Carlyle, Sartor Resartus

It is almost a definition of a gentleman to say
that he is one who never inflicts pain.

John Henry Cardinal Newman, The Idea of a University

A man is a god in ruins.

Ralph Waldo Emerson, Nature

Fine manners need the support of fine manners in others.

Ralph Waldo Emerson, The Conduct of Life

Life is not so short but that there is
always time enough for courtesy.

Ralph Waldo Emerson, Letters and Social Aims

Some people are so fond of ill luck that
they run halfway to meet it.

Douglas Jerrold, Wit and Opinions of Douglas Jerrold

Little things affect little minds.

Benjamin Disraeli, Earl of Beaconsfield, Sybil; or, The Two Nations

Keep yourself to yourself.

Charles Dickens, Pickwick Papers

There is a passion for hunting something
deeply implanted in the human breast.

Charles Dickens, Oliver Twist

Subdue your appetites, my dears, and
you've conquered human nature.

Charles Dickens, Nicholas Nickleby

Any man may be in good spirits and good temper when
he's well dressed. There ain't much credit in that.

Charles Dickens, Martin Chuzzlewit

Keep up appearances whatever you do.

Charles Dickens, Martin Chuzzlewit

Never . . . be mean in anything;
never be false; never be cruel.

Charles Dickens, David Copperfield

Accidents will occur in the best-regulated families.

Charles Dickens, David Copperfield

A wonderful fact to reflect upon, that every human
creature is constituted to be that profound
secret and mystery to every other.

Charles Dickens, A Tale of Two Cities

The savage in man is never quite eradicated.

Henry David Thoreau, Journal

The mass of men lead lives of quiet desperation. What is
called resignation is confirmed desperation.

Henry David Thoreau, Walden

For as this appalling ocean surrounds the verdant land,
so in the soul of man there lies one insular Tahiti,
full of peace and joy, but encompassed by all
the horrors of the half known life.

Herman Melville, Moby-Dick

Conduct is three-fourths of our life and its largest concern.

Matthew Arnold, Literature and Dogma

There is no feeling in a human heart which exists
in that heart alone — which is not, in some
form or degree, in every heart.

George Macdonald, Unspoken Sermons

What a woman thinks of women is the test of her nature.
George Meredith, Diana of the Crossways

Happy families are all alike; every unhappy
family is unhappy in its own way.
Leo Nikolaevich Tolstoi, Anna Karenina

Man is the only animal that blushes. Or needs to.
Mark Twain, Following the Equator

Knowledge of human nature is the beginning
and end of political education.
Henry Adams, The Education of Henry Adams

An unlearned carpenter of my acquaintance once said in
my hearing: "There is very little difference between one
man and another; but what little there is, is very important."
This distinction seems to me to go to the root of the matter.
William James, The Will to Believe

Cats and monkeys, monkeys and cats —
all human life is there.
Henry James, The Madonna of the Future

Distrust all in whom the impulse to punish is powerful.
Friedrich Wilhelm Nietzsche, Thus Spake Zarathustra

Tact is after all a kind of mind-reading.

Sarah Orne Jewett, The Country of the Pointed Firs

Conversation . . . is the art of never appearing a bore, of knowing how to say everything interestingly, to entertain with no matter what, to be charming with nothing at all.

Guy de Maupassant, Sur l'Eau (On the Water)

What is a cynic? A man who knows the price of everything, and the value of nothing.

Oscar Wilde, Lady Windermere's Fan

Only in men's imagination does every truth find an effective and undeniable existence. Imagination, not invention, is the supreme master of art as of life.

Joseph Conrad, A Personal Record

Man is a successful animal, that's all.

Remy de Gourmont, Promenades Philosophiques

Never praise a sister to a sister, in the hope of your compliments reaching the proper ears.

Rudyard Kipling, Plain Tales from the Hills

Men are always sincere. They change sincerities, that's all.

Tristan Bernard, Ce Que l'On Dit aux Femmes

Pessimism, when you get used to it,
is just as agreeable as optimism.
Arnold Bennett, Things That Have Interested Me

Of courtesy, it is much less
Than courage of heart or holiness,
Yet in my walks it seems to me
That the Grace of God is in courtesy.
Hilaire Belloc, Courtesy

Home is the place where, when you have to go there,
They have to take you in.
Robert Frost, The Death of the Hired Man

The greatest thing in family life is to take a hint
when a hint is intended — and not to take
a hint when a hint isn't intended.
Robert Frost, Comment

I am myself and what is around me, and if I
do not save it, it shall not save me.
José Ortega y Gasset, Meditations on Quixote

I never saw a wild thing
Sorry for itself.
D. H. Lawrence, Self-Pity

Modesty and unselfishness — these are virtues
which men praise — and pass by.

André Maurois, Ariel

Among animals, one has a sense of humor.
Humor saves a few steps, it saves years.

Marianne Moore, The Pangolin

Dreams are necessary to life.

Anaïs Nin, The Diary of Anaïs Nin, II

Human beings are perhaps never more frightening than
when they are convinced beyond doubt that they are right.

Laurens Van der Post, The Lost World of the Kalahari

That's it, baby, if you've got it, flaunt it.

Mel Brooks, The Producers

A healthy male adult consumes each year one and a half
times his own weight in other people's patience.

John Updike, Assorted Prose

We are cruel enough without meaning to be.

John Updike, Rabbit Is Rich

We are an intelligent species and the use of our intelligence quite properly gives us pleasure. In this respect the brain is like a muscle. When it is in use we feel very good. Understanding is joyous.

Carl Sagan, Broca's Brain

Don't cross the bridge until you come to it.

Anonymous, Proverb

Law and Justice

Do justice, that you may live long upon earth. Calm the
weeper, do not oppress the widow, do not oust a man
from his father's property, do not degrade magnates
from their seats. Beware of punishing wrongfully;
do not kill, for it will not profit you.

The Teaching for Merikare, Parable

Thou shalt not take the name of the Lord thy God in vain.
Remember the sabbath day, to keep it holy.
Six days shalt thou labor, and do all thy work:
But the seventh day . . . thou shalt not do any work . . .
Honor thy father and thy mother: that thy days may be long
upon the land which the Lord thy God giveth thee.
Thou shalt not kill.
Thou shalt not commit adultery.
Thou shalt not steal.
Thou shalt not bear false witness against thy neighbor.
Thou shalt not covet thy neighbor's house, thou shalt
not covet thy neighbor's wife, nor his manservant,
nor his maidservant, nor his ox, nor his ass,
nor any thing that is thy neighbor's.

The Bible, Exodus

Judge not, that ye be not judged.

The Bible, Matthew

Love is the fulfilling of the law.

The Bible, The Epistle of Paul the Apostle to the Romans

If you know that [a] thing is unrighteous, then use all dispatch in putting an end to it — why wait till next year?

Mencius, Works

To be turned from one's course by men's opinions,
by blame, and by misrepresentation shows
a man unfit to hold an office.

Quintus Fabius Maximus, From Plutarch, Lives

Extreme law is often extreme injustice.

Terence, Heauton Timoroumenos

Let the punishment match the offense.

Marcus Tullius Cicero, De Legibus

Had I a hundred tongues, a hundred mouths, a voice of
iron and a chest of brass, I could not tell all the forms of
crime, could not name all the types of punishment.

Virgil, Aeneid

Law: an ordinance of reason for the common good, made
by him who has care of the community.

Saint Thomas Aquinas, Summa Theologica

What can only be taught by the rod and with blows will
not lead to much good; they will not remain pious
any longer than the rod is behind them.

Martin Luther, The Great Catechism

Revenge is a kind of wild justice, which the more man's
nature runs to, the more ought law to weed it out.

Francis Bacon, Essays

The abuse of greatness is when it disjoins
Remorse from power.

William Shakespeare, Julius Caesar

Ignorance of the law excuses no man; not that all men
know the law, but because 'tis an excuse every man will
plead, and no man can tell how to refute him.

John Webster, Table Talk

Only the actions of the just
Smell sweet and blossom in their dust.

James Shirley, The Lady of Pleasure

Give me the liberty to know, to utter, and to argue freely
according to conscience, above all liberties.

John Milton, Areopagitica

The love of justice in most men is simply
the fear of suffering injustice.

François, Duc de La Rochefoucauld, Reflections

The end must justify the means.

Matthew Prior, Hans Carvel

Laws are like cobwebs, which may catch small flies,
but let wasps and hornets break through.

Jonathan Swift, A Critical Essay upon the Faculties of the Mind

Liberty is the right of doing whatever the laws permit.

Charles de Secondat, Baron de Montesquieu, De l'Esprit des Lois

He who is merely just is severe.

Voltaire, Letter to Frederick the Great

It is better to risk saving a guilty person than
to condemn an innocent one.

Voltaire, Zadig

Unlimited power is apt to corrupt the minds of those
who possess it; and this I know, my lords, that
where laws end, tyranny begins.

William Pitt, Earl of Chatham, Case of Wilkes

It is better that ten guilty persons
escape than one innocent suffer.

Sir William Blackstone, Commentaries

Is life so dear or peace so sweet as to be purchased at
the price of chains and slavery? Forbid it, Almighty God.
I know not what course others may take, but as
for me, give me liberty or give me death!

Patrick Henry, Speech in Virginia Convention, Richmond

The sword of justice has no scabbard.

Joseph de Maistre, Les Soirées de Saint-Petersbourg

It is justice, not charity, that is wanting in the world.

Mary Wollstonecraft, A Vindication of the Rights of Woman

Decision by majorities is as much an
expedient as lighting by gas.

William Ewart Gladstone, Speech in the House of Commons

Justice delayed is justice denied.

William Ewart Gladstone, Attributed

Any people anywhere, being inclined and having the power, have the right to rise up, and shake off the existing government, and form a new one that suits them better.

Abraham Lincoln, Speech in the House of Representatives

No man is good enough to govern another man without that other's consent.

Abraham Lincoln, Speech at Peoria, Illinois

As I would not be a slave, so I would not be a master. This expresses my idea of democracy. Whatever differs from this, to the extent of the difference, is no democracy.

Abraham Lincoln, From Roy P. Basler,
The Collected Works of Abraham Lincoln

Let us have faith that right makes might, and in that faith let us to the end dare to do our duty as we understand it.

Abraham Lincoln, Address at Cooper Union, New York

This country, with its institutions, belongs to the people who inhabit it. Whenever they shall grow weary of the existing government, they can exercise their constitutional right of amending it, or their revolutionary right to dismember or overthrow it.

Abraham Lincoln, First Inaugural Address

The best use of laws is to teach men to
trample bad laws under their feet.
Wendell Phillips, Speech

In the little world in which children have their existence,
whosoever brings them up, there is nothing so finely
perceived and so finely felt, as injustice.
Charles Dickens, Great Expectations

Politics is the art of the possible.
Otto von Bismarck, Remark

Under a government which imprisons any unjustly, the true
place for a just man is also a prison . . . the only house in a
slave State in which a free man can abide with honor.
Henry David Thoreau, Civil Disobedience

No man can put a chain about the ankle of his
fellow man without at last finding the other
end fastened about his own neck.
Frederick Douglass, Speech at Civil Rights Mass Meeting, Washington, D.C.

Where justice is denied, where poverty is enforced,
where ignorance prevails, and where any one class
is made to feel that society is in an organized
conspiracy to oppress, rob, and degrade them,
neither persons nor property will be safe.

*Frederick Douglass, Speech on the twenty-fourth anniversary of
Emancipation in the District of Columbia, Washington, D.C.*

Our Constitution is color-blind, and neither knows nor
tolerates classes among citizens. In respect of civil
rights, all citizens are equal before the law. The
humblest is the peer of the most powerful.

John Marshall Harlan, Dissenting opinion, Plessy v. Ferguson

Power tends to corrupt and absolute
power corrupts absolutely.

*John Emerich Edward Dalberg-Acton, Lord Acton,
Letter to Bishop Mandell Creighton*

No man is above the law and no man is below it;
nor do we ask any man's permission when we
require him to obey it. Obedience to the law
is demanded as a right; not asked as a favor.

Theodore Roosevelt, Third Annual Message

Hogan's r-right whin he says: "Justice is blind."
Blind she is, an' deef an' dumb an' has a wooden leg.

Finley Peter Dunne, Mr. Dooley's Opinions

Justice is a machine that, when someone has once
given it the starting push, rolls on of itself.
John Galsworthy, Justice

The law must be stable, but it must not stand still.
Roscoe Pound, Introduction to the Philosophy of Law

Every race and every nation should be judged by the
best it has been able to produce, not by the worst.
James Weldon Johnson, The Autobiography of an Ex-Colored Man

Injustice is relatively easy to bear; what stings is justice.
H. L. Mencken, Prejudices

Don't get mad, get even.
Joseph Kennedy, Attributed

As soon as men decide that all means are permitted to fight
an evil, then their good becomes indistinguishable
from the evil that they set out to destroy.
Christopher Dawson, The Judgment of the Nations

Outside the kingdom of the Lord there is no nation
which is greater than any other. God and
history will remember your judgment.
Haile Selassie, Speech, the League of Nations

The death of democracy is not likely to be an assassination
from ambush. It will be a slow extinction from
apathy, indifference, and undernourishment.

Robert Maynard Hutchins, Great Books

I had felt for a long time, that if I was ever told to get up so
a white person could sit, that I would refuse to do so.

Rosa Parks, Recalling her refusal to give up her seat on a Montgomery,
Alabama, bus

I have fought against white domination, and I have fought
against black domination. I have cherished the ideal of a
democratic and free society in which all persons will
live together in harmony and with equal opportunities.
It is an ideal which I hope to live for and achieve. But, if
needs be, it is an ideal for which I am prepared to die.

Nelson Mandela, Statement in the dock

I have spent all my life under a Communist regime, and I
will tell you that a society without any objective legal scale
is a terrible one indeed. But a society with no other scale
but the legal one is not quite worthy of man either.

Alexander Isayevich Solzhenitsyn, The Exhausted West

Whether we bring our enemies to justice, or bring
justice to our enemies, justice will be done.

George W. Bush, Address to joint session of Congress

Love and Marriage

It is not good that the man should be alone;
I will make him an help meet for him.
The Bible, The First Book of Moses, Called Genesis

Whoso findeth a wife findeth a good thing.
The Bible, The Proverbs

Many waters cannot quench love,
neither can the floods drown it.
The Bible, The Song of Solomon

Her sins, which are many, are forgiven; for she loved much.
The Bible, The Gospel According to Saint Luke

One word
Frees us of all the weight and pain of life:
That word is love.
Sophocles, Oedipus at Colonus

Marriage, if one will face the truth, is an evil,
but a necessary evil.
Menander, Unidentified fragment

Lovers' quarrels are the renewal of love.

Terence, Andria

I know the disposition of women: when you will,
they won't; when you won't, they set their
hearts upon you of their own inclination.

Terence, Eunuchus

Let us live and love, my Lesbia, and value at a penny all the
talk of crabbed old men. Suns may set and rise again: for
us, when our brief light has set, there's the sleep of
perpetual night. Give me a thousand kisses.

Gaius Valerius Catullus, Carmina

What a woman says to her ardent lover should
be written in wind and running water.

Gaius Valerius Catullus, Carmina

Love conquers all things; let us too surrender to Love.

Virgil, Eclogues

Happy, thrice happy and more, are they whom an
unbroken bond unites and whose love shall know
no sundering quarrels so long as they shall live.

Horace, Odes

Never change when love has found its home.
Sextus Propertius, Elegies

Love yields to business. If you seek a way out of love,
be busy; you'll be safe then.
Ovid, Remedia Amoris

It is easier to mend neglect than to quicken love.
Saint Jerome, Letter 7

Love knows nothing of order.
Saint Jerome, Letter 7

Love kindled by virtue always kindles another,
provided that its flame appear outwardly.
Dante Alighieri, The Divine Comedy

To be able to say how much you love is to love but little.
Petrarch, To Laura in Death

Hard is the herte that loveth nought
In May.
Geoffrey Chaucer, The Romaunt of the Rose

For love is blynd.
Geoffrey Chaucer, The Canterbury Tales

Be not angry that you cannot make others as
you wish them to be, since you cannot
make yourself as you wish to be.
Thomas à Kempis, Imitation of Christ

Love is swift, sincere, pious, pleasant, gentle, strong,
patient, faithful, prudent, long-suffering, manly and
never seeking her own; for wheresoever a man
seeketh his own, there he falleth from love.
Thomas à Kempis, Imitation of Christ

It is easier to resist at the beginning than at the end.
Leonardo da Vinci, The Notebooks

Since love and fear can hardly exist together, if we must
choose between them, it is far safer to be feared than loved.
Niccolò Machiavelli, The Prince

There is no more lovely, friendly and charming relationship,
communion or company than a good marriage.
Martin Luther, Table Talk

Wedding is destiny,
And hanging likewise.
John Heywood, Proverbs

Remember the old saying, "Faint heart ne'er won fair lady."
Miguel de Cervantes, Don Quixote

Love and War are the same thing, and stratagems and
policy are as allowable in the one as in the other.
Miguel de Cervantes, Don Quixote

Who ever loved that loved not at first sight?
Christopher Marlowe, Hero and Leander

Hasty marriage seldom proveth well.
William Shakespeare, King Henry the Sixth, Part III

Kindness in women, not their beauteous looks,
Shall win my love.
William Shakespeare, The Taming of the Shrew

What's in a name? that which we call a rose
By any other name would smell as sweet.
William Shakespeare, Romeo and Juliet

Therefore love moderately; long love doth so;
Too swift arrives as tardy as too slow.

William Shakespeare, Romeo and Juliet

Men have died from time to time, and worms
have eaten them, but not for love.

William Shakespeare, As You Like It

The kiss you take is better than you give.

William Shakespeare, Troilus and Cressida

If music be the food of love, play on.

William Shakespeare, Twelfth-Night

Shall I compare thee to a summer's day?
Thou art more lovely and more temperate:
Rough winds do shake the darling buds of May,
And summer's lease hath all too short a date.

William Shakespeare, Sonnet 18

And ruin'd love, when it is built anew,
Grows fairer than at first, more strong, far greater.

William Shakespeare, Sonnet 119

Oh do not die, for I shall hate
All women so, when thou art gone.

John Donne, A Fever

Love built on beauty, soon as beauty, dies.

John Donne, Elegies

So dear I love him, that with him all deaths
I could endure, without him live no life.

John Milton, Paradise Lost

She that with poetry is won
Is but a desk to write upon.

Samuel Butler, Hudibras

There is no disguise which can for long conceal love
where it exists or simulate it where it does not.

François, Duc de La Rochefoucauld, Reflections

The mind is always the dupe of the heart.

François, Duc de La Rochefoucauld, Reflections

As lines, so loves oblique, may well
Themselves in every angle greet;
But ours, so truly parallel,
Though infinite, can never meet.
Therefore the love which us doth bind
But fate so enviously debars,
Is the conjunction of the mind,
And opposition of the stars.

Andrew Marvell, The Definition of Love

Married in haste, we may repent at leisure.

William Congreve, The Old Bachelor

Heaven has no rage like love to hatred turned,
Nor hell a fury like a woman scorned.

William Congreve, The Mourning Bride

What dire offense from amorous causes springs,
What mighty contests rise from trivial things!

Alexander Pope, The Rape of the Lock

Where there's marriage without love, there
will be love without marriage.

Benjamin Franklin, Poor Richard's Almanac

Love and scandal are the best sweeteners of tea.

Henry Fielding, Love in Several Masques

If I love you, what business is it of yours?
Johann Wolfgang von Goethe, Wilhelm Meister's Apprenticeship

The sum which two married people owe to one
another defies calculation. It is an infinite debt, which
can only be discharged through all eternity.
Johann Wolfgang von Goethe, Elective Affinities

'Tis safest in matrimony to begin with a little aversion.
Richard Brinsley Sheridan, The Rivals

Through all the drama — whether damned or not —
Love gilds the scene, and women guide the plot.
Richard Brinsley Sheridan, The Rivals

Love is the whole history of a woman's life,
it is but an episode in a man's.
Germaine de Staël, De l'Influence des Passions

In peace, Love tunes the shepherd's reed;
In war, he mounts the warrior's steed;
In halls, in gay attire is seen;
In hamlets, dances on the green.
Love rules the court, the camp, the grove,
And men below, and saints above;
For love is heaven, and heaven is love.
Sir Walter Scott, The Lay of the Last Minstrel

Marriage resembles a pair of shears, so joined that they can
not be separated; often moving in opposite directions, yet
always punishing anyone who comes between them.

Sydney Smith, Lady Holland's Memoir

All thoughts, all passions, all delights,
Whatever stirs this mortal frame,
All are but ministers of Love,
And feed his sacred flame.

Samuel Taylor Coleridge, Love

The man's desire is for the woman; but the woman's desire
is rarely other than for the desire of the man.

Samuel Taylor Coleridge, Table Talk

A lady's imagination is very rapid; it jumps from admiration
to love, from love to matrimony in a moment.

Jane Austen, Pride and Prejudice

To marry is to halve your rights and double your duties.

Arthur Schopenhauer, The World as Will and Idea

Familiar acts are beautiful through love.

Percy Bysshe Shelley, Prometheus Unbound

It is easier to be a lover than a husband for the simple
reason that it is more difficult to be witty every day
than to say pretty things from time to time.

Honoré de Balzac, Physiologie du Mariage

Our heart is a treasury; if you spend all its
wealth at once you are ruined.

Honoré de Balzac, Le Père Goriot

Let men tremble to win the hand of woman, unless they
win along with it the utmost passion of her heart.

Nathaniel Hawthorne, The Scarlet Letter

There is only one happiness in life, to love and be loved.

George Sand, Letter to Lina Calamatta

How do I love thee? Let me count the ways.
I love thee to the depth and breadth and height
My soul can reach, when feeling out of sight
For the ends of Being and ideal Grace.

Elizabeth Barrett Browning, Sonnets from the Portuguese

Two souls with but a single thought,
Two hearts that beat as one.

Friedrich Halm, Der Sohn der Wildness

Oh heart! oh blood that freezes, blood that burns!
Earth's returns
For whole centuries of folly, noise and sin!
Shut them in,
With their triumphs and their glories and the rest!
Love is best!

Robert Browning, Love Among the Ruins

Only I discern
Infinite passion, and the pain
Of finite hearts that yearn.

Robert Browning, Two in the Campagna

There is no road to wealth so easy and
respectable as that of matrimony.

Anthony Trollope, Doctor Thorne

The human heart has hidden treasures,
In secret kept, in silence sealed.

Charlotte Brontë, Evening Solace

Love iz like the meazles; we kant have it bad but onst, and
the later in life we have it the tuffer it goes with us.

Josh Billings, His Sayings

Of all the icy blasts that blow on love, a request for money
is the most chilling and havoc-wreaking.

Gustave Flaubert, Madame Bovary

A Woman is a foreign land,
Of which, though there he settle young,
A man will ne'er quite understand
The customs, politics, and tongue.

Coventry Patmore, The Angel in the House

A lover without indiscretion is no lover at all.

Thomas Hardy, The Hand of Ethelberta

The fundamental error of their matrimonial union; that of
having based a permanent contract on a temporary feeling.

Thomas Hardy, Jude the Obscure

A tale without love is like beef without mustard: insipid.

Anatole France, The Revolt of the Angels

Love is the state in which man sees things most widely
different from what they are. The force of illusion
reaches its zenith here, as likewise the sweetening and
transfiguring power. When a man is in love he endures
more than at other times; he submits to everything.

Friedrich Wilhelm Nietzsche, The Antichrist

Here are fruits, flowers, leaves and branches,
And here is my heart which beats only for you.

Paul Verlaine, Romances sans Paroles

Love is . . . born with the pleasure of looking at each other,
it is fed with the necessity of seeing each other, it is
concluded with the impossibility of separation!

José Martí, Amor

The awe and dread with which the untutored savage
contemplates his mother-in-law are amongst the
most familiar facts of anthropology.

Sir James George Frazer, The Golden Bough

The fickleness of the women I love is only equaled by
the infernal constancy of the women who love me.

George Bernard Shaw, The Philanderer

When two people are under the influence of the most
violent, most insane, most delusive, and most transient of
passions, they are required to swear that they will remain
in that excited, abnormal, and exhausting condition
continuously until death do them part.

George Bernard Shaw, Getting Married

A pity beyond all telling
Is hid in the heart of love.

William Butler Yeats, The Rose

Hearts are not had as a gift but hearts are earned.

William Butler Yeats, Michael Robartes and the Dancer

No man has ever lived that had enough
Of children's gratitude or woman's love.
William Butler Yeats, The Winding Stair and Other Poems

One of the best things about love is just recognizing a
man's step when he climbs the stairs.
Colette, Occupation

Love consists in this, that two solitudes protect
and touch and greet each other.
Rainer Maria Rilke, Letters to a Young Poet

A good marriage is that in which each
appoints the other guardian of his solitude.
Rainer Maria Rilke, Letters

Man and woman are two locked caskets, of which
each contains the key to the other.
Isak Dinesen, Winter Tales

What is love? . . . It is the morning and the evening star.
Sinclair Lewis, Elmer Gantry

Hell, Madame, is to love no longer.
*Georges Bernanos, Le Journal d'un Curé de
Campagne (The Diary of a Country Priest)*

The critical period in matrimony is breakfasttime.
Sir Alan Patrick Herbert, Uncommon Law

Marriage . . . is a damnably serious business,
particularly around Boston.
John P. Marquand, The Late George Apley

Even memory is not necessary for love. There is a land
of the living and a land of the dead and the bridge
is love, the only survival, the only meaning.
Thornton Wilder, The Bridge of San Luis Rey

Love does not consist in gazing at each other but in looking
outward together in the same direction.
Antoine de Saint-Exupéry, Wind, Sand and Stars

In every house of marriage
there's room for an interpreter.
Stanley Kunitz, Route Six

He was my North, my South, my East and West,
My working week and my Sunday rest,
My noon, my midnight, my talk, my song;
I thought that love would last forever: I was wrong.
W. H. Auden, Twelve Songs

Like love we don't know where or why
Like love we can't compel or fly
Like love we often weep
Like love we seldom keep.

W. H. Auden, Law Like Love

[Sex:] The most fun I've ever had without laughing.

Woody Allen, Annie Hall

Love means not ever having to say you're sorry.

Erich Segal, Love Story

We've been married for twenty-two years. And I have
learned a long time ago that the only two people who
count in any marriage are the two who are in it.

Hillary Rodham Clinton, The Today show

Everybody lies about sex. People lie during sex.
If it weren't for lies, there'd be no sex.

Jerry Seinfeld, New York Times

It's love, it's love that makes the world go round.

Anonymous, French song

Nature

But ask now the beasts, and they shall teach thee; and the
fowls of the air, and they shall tell thee:
Or speak to the earth, and it shall teach thee; and the fishes
of the sea shall declare unto thee.

The Bible, The Book of Job

Hath the rain a father? or who hath
begotten the drops of dew?

The Bible, The Book of Job

The desert shall rejoice, and blossom as the rose.

The Bible, The Book of the Prophet Isaiah

Who can number the sand of the sea,
and the drops of rain, and the days of eternity?

*The Bible, The Apocrypha, The Wisdom of Jesus
the Son of Sirach, or Ecclesiasticus*

Nothing endures but change.

Heraclitus, From Diogenes Laertius, Lives of Eminent Philosophers

In all things of nature there is something of the marvelous.

Aristotle, On the Parts of Animals

Nature does nothing uselessly.

Aristotle, Politics

The goal of life is living in agreement with nature.

Zeno, From Diogenes Laertius, Lives of Eminent Philosophers

You may drive out Nature with a pitchfork,
yet she still will hurry back.

Horace, Epistles

All art is but imitation of nature.

Lucius Annaeus Seneca, Epistles

All that is harmony for you, my Universe, is in harmony
with me as well. Nothing that comes at the right time for
you is too early or too late for me. Everything is fruit to me
that your seasons bring, Nature. All things come of you,
have their being in you, and return to you.

Marcus Aurelius Antoninus, Meditations

You will find something more in woods than
in books. Trees and stones will teach you that
which you can never learn from masters.

Saint Bernard, Epistle

In the realm of Nature there is nothing
purposeless, trivial, or unnecessary.

Maimonides, The Guide for the Perplexed

Human subtlety . . . will never devise an invention
more beautiful, more simple or more direct than
does nature, because in her inventions nothing
is lacking, and nothing is superfluous.

Leonardo da Vinci, The Notebooks

Let us give Nature a chance; she knows
her business better than we do.

Michel Eyquem de Montaigne, Essays

Nature is often hidden; sometimes overcome;
seldom extinguished.

Francis Bacon, Essays

The heart of animals is the foundation of their life,
the sovereign of everything within them,
the sun of their microcosm.

William Harvey, De Motu Cordis et Sanguinis

By viewing Nature, Nature's handmaid Art,
Makes mighty things from small beginnings grow.
John Dryden, Annus Mirabilis

Nature abhors a vacuum.
Benedict Spinoza, Ethics

After a storm comes a calm.
Matthew Henry, Commentaries

Gie me ae spark o' Nature's fire,
That's a' the learning I desire.
Robert Burns, First Epistle to J. Lapraik

Come forth into the light of things,
Let Nature be your teacher.
William Wordsworth, The Tables Turned

Nature is full of genius, full of the divinity; so that not a
snowflake escapes its fashioning hand.
Henry David Thoreau, Journal

In wildness is the preservation of the world.
Henry David Thoreau, Walking

If we had a keen vision of all that is ordinary in human life,
it would be like hearing the grass grow or the
squirrel's heart beat, and we should die of that
roar which is the other side of silence.

George Eliot, Middlemarch

There is nothing so desperately monotonous as the sea,
and I no longer wonder at the cruelty of pirates.

James Russell Lowell, Fireside Travels

I believe a leaf of grass is no less than
the journey-work of the stars.

Walt Whitman, Song of Myself

What is life? It is the flash of a firefly in the night. It is the
breath of a buffalo in the wintertime. It is the little shadow
which runs across the grass and loses itself in the sunset.

Crowfoot, Last words

Nature, with equal mind,
Sees all her sons at play;
Sees man control the wind,
The wind sweep man away.

Matthew Arnold, Empedocles on Etna

Everybody talks about the weather,
but nobody does anything about it.

Mark Twain, Attributed

Nature teaches more than she preaches. There are
no sermons in stones. It is easier to get a
spark out of a stone than a moral.

John Burroughs, Time and Change

The clearest way into the Universe is
through a forest wilderness.

John Muir, John of the Mountains

Summer afternoon — summer afternoon; to me
those have always been the two most beautiful
words in the English language.

Henry James, Quoted by Edith Wharton, A Backward Glance

To waste, to destroy, our natural resources, to skin and
exhaust the land instead of using it so as to increase its
usefulness, will result in undermining in the days of our
children the very prosperity which we ought by right
to hand down to them amplified and developed.

Theodore Roosevelt, Message to Congress

I hate to see the evenin' sun go down.

W. C. Handy, The St. Louis Blues

How many times it thundered before Franklin took the hint!
How many apples fell on Newton's head before he took
the hint! Nature is always hinting at us. It hints over
and over again. And suddenly we take the hint.

Robert Frost, Comment

Nature is trying very hard to make us succeed, but nature
does not depend on us. We are not the only experiment.

R. Buckminster Fuller, Interview in the Minneapolis Tribune

Nature, Mr. Allnut, is what we are put
into this world to rise above.

James Agee, The African Queen

We are the children of our landscape; it dictates
behavior and even thought in the measure to which
we are responsive to it.

Lawrence Durrell, Justine

The world where the owl is endlessly hungry and endlessly
on the hunt is the world in which I live too.

Mary Oliver, Blue Pastures

Though I have looked everywhere
I can find nothing lowly
in the universe.

A. R. Ammons, Still

I think it pisses God off if you walk by the color
purple in a field somewhere and don't notice it.

Alice Walker, The Color Purple

Peace and War

Wickedness proceedeth from the wicked.
The Bible, The First Book of Samuel

Mark the perfect man, and behold the upright:
for the end of that man is peace.
The Bible, The Book of Psalms

The words of his mouth were smoother than butter,
but war was in his heart: his words were softer
than oil, yet were they drawn swords.
The Bible, The Book of Psalms

Peace be within thy walls, and prosperity
within thy palaces.
The Bible, The Book of Psalms

He that is slow to anger is better than the mighty; and he
that ruleth his spirit than he that taketh a city.
The Bible, The Proverbs

They shall beat their swords into plowshares, and their spears into pruninghooks: nation shall not lift up sword against nation, neither shall they learn war any more.

The Bible, The Book of the Prophet Isaiah

There is no peace, saith the Lord, unto the wicked.

The Bible, The Book of the Prophet Isaiah

How beautiful upon the mountains are the feet of him that bringeth good tidings, that publisheth peace.

The Bible, The Book of the Prophet Isaiah

And when they are in their cups, they forget their love both to friends and brethren, and a little after draw out swords.

The Bible, The Apocrypha, I Esdras

Love your enemies, bless them that curse you, do good to them that hate you, and pray for them which despitefully use you, and persecute you.

The Bible, Matthew

He that is not with me is against me.

The Bible, Matthew

All they that take the sword shall perish with the sword.

The Bible, Matthew

When armies are mobilized and issues joined,
The man who is sorry over the fact will win.
Lao-tzu, The Way of Lao-tzu

Hatred does not cease by hatred at any time:
hatred ceases by love — this is the eternal law.
The Pali Canon, Suttapitaka

In peace, children inter their parents; war violates the order
of nature and causes parents to inter their children.
Herodotus, Histories

A military operation involves deception. Even though
you are competent, appear to be incompetent.
Though effective, appear to be ineffective.
Sun-tzu, The Art of War

Victorious warriors win first and then go to war, while
defeated warriors go to war first and then seek to win.
Sun-tzu, The Art of War

Be extremely subtle, even to the point of formlessness.
Be extremely mysterious, even to the point
of soundlessness. Thereby you can be
the director of the opponent's fate.
Sun-tzu, The Art of War

He is wise who tries everything before arms.

Terence, Eunuchus

Law stands mute in the midst of arms.

Marcus Tullius Cicero, Pro Milone

We are mad, not only individually, but nationally. We check
manslaughter and isolated murders; but what of war and
the much vaunted crime of slaughtering whole peoples?

Lucius Annaeus Seneca, Epistles

Let him who desires peace prepare for war.

Vegetius, De Rei Militari

First keep the peace within yourself, then you
can also bring peace to others.

Thomas à Kempis, Imitation of Christ

A prince should therefore have no other aim or thought,
nor take up any other thing for his study, but war and
its organization and discipline, for that is the only art
that is necessary to one who commands.

Niccolò Machiavelli, The Prince

War begun without good provision of money beforehand
for going through with it is but as a breathing of
strength and blast that will quickly pass away.
Coin is the sinews of war.

François Rabelais, Gargantua and Pantagruel

Blessed are the peacemakers on earth.

William Shakespeare, King Henry the Sixth, Part II

Who overcomes
By force hath overcome but half his foe.

John Milton, Paradise Lost

War seldom enters but where wealth allures.

John Dryden, The Hind and the Panther

Peace is not an absence of war, it is a virtue, a state of
mind, a disposition for benevolence, confidence, justice.

Benedict Spinoza, Theological-Political Treatise

Do not men die fast enough without being destroyed by
each other? Can any man be insensible of the brevity of life?
and can he who knows it, think life too long?

François de Salignac de la Mothe Fénelon, Télémaque

A patriot is a fool in ev'ry age.

Alexander Pope, Imitations of Horace

Don't throw stones at your neighbors',
if your own windows are glass.

Benjamin Franklin, Poor Richard's Almanac

There never was a good war or a bad peace.

Benjamin Franklin, Letter to Josiah Quincy

War is much too serious a matter to
be entrusted to the military.

Charles Maurice de Talleyrand-Périgord, Attributed

War nourishes war.

Johann Friedrich von Schiller, The Piccolomini

Nothing except a battle lost can be half
so melancholy as a battle won.

Arthur Wellesley, Duke of Wellington, Dispatch from the field of Waterloo

The surest way to prevent war is not to fear it.

John Randolph, Speech in the House of Representatives

Beneath the rule of men entirely great,
The pen is mightier than the sword.

Edward Bulwer-Lytton, Baron Lytton, Richelieu

It is well that war is so terrible, or
we should grow too fond of it.

Robert E. Lee, On seeing a Federal charge repulsed at Fredericksburg

All your strength is in your union.
All your danger is in discord;
Therefore be at peace henceforward,
And as brothers live together.

Henry Wadsworth Longfellow, The Song of Hiawatha

If we could read the secret history of our enemies,
we should find in each man's life sorrow and
suffering enough to disarm all hostility.

Henry Wadsworth Longfellow, Driftwood

Force is not a remedy.

John Bright, Speech at Birmingham

Ef you want peace, the thing you've gut tu du
Is jes' to show you're up to fightin', tu.

James Russell Lowell, The Biglow Papers

All wars are boyish, and are fought by boys.

Herman Melville, Battle-Pieces

War is at best barbarism. . . . Its glory is all moonshine. It is
only those who have neither fired a shot nor heard the
shrieks and groans of the wounded who cry aloud for
blood, more vengeance, more desolation. War is hell.

William Tecumseh Sherman, Attributed to a
graduation address at Michigan Military Academy

It is easier to make war than peace.

Georges Clemenceau, Speech

It must be a peace without victory. . . .
Only a peace between equals can last.

Woodrow Wilson, Address to the Senate

All civilization has from time to time become a
thin crust over a volcano of revolution.

Havelock Ellis, Little Essays of Love and Virtue

A man may build himself a throne of bayonets,
but he cannot sit on it.

William Ralph Inge, From Wit and Wisdom of Dean Inge,
edited by Marchant

The deliberate aim at Peace very easily passes
into its bastard substitute, Anesthesia.

Alfred North Whitehead, Adventures of Ideas

In War: Resolution. In Defeat: Defiance.
In Victory: Magnanimity. In Peace: Good Will.

Sir Winston Spencer Churchill, The Second World War: Moral of the Work

If a nation values anything more than freedom, it will lose
its freedom; and the irony of it is that if it is comfort or
money that it values more, it will lose that too.

W. Somerset Maugham, Strictly Personal

Peace, it's wonderful.

Father Divine, Motto of the Peace Mission Movement

More than an end to war, we want an end
to the beginnings of all wars.

Franklin Delano Roosevelt, Address written for Jefferson Day broadcast

Wars may be fought with weapons, but they are won
by men. It is the spirit of the men who follow and
of the man who leads that gains the victory.

George S. Patton, In the Cavalry Journal

You have to take chances for peace, just as you must
take chances in war. . . . The ability to get to the verge
without getting into the war is the necessary art.
If you try to run away from it, if you are scared
to go to the brink, you are lost.

John Foster Dulles, From James Shepley,
How Dulles Averted War, in Life

In war there is no second prize for the runner-up.

Omar Bradley, In the Military Review

What use bombs and antibombs,
Sovereign powers, brutal lives, ugly deaths?
Are men born to go down like this?

Jean Toomer, The Blue Meridian

If we win here we will win everywhere. The world is
a fine place and worth the fighting for and
I hate very much to leave it.

Ernest Hemingway, For Whom the Bell Tolls

Although human life is priceless, we always act as if
something had an even greater price than life. . . .
But what is that something?

Antoine de Saint-Exupéry, Night Flight

There are no atheists in the foxholes.

William Thomas Cummings, Field sermon, Bataan

You know — we've had to imagine the war here,
and we have imagined that it was being fought
by aging men like ourselves. We had forgotten that
wars were fought by babies. When I saw those
freshly shaved faces, it was a shock. "My God, my
God —" I said to myself, "it's the Children's Crusade."

Kurt Vonnegut, Slaughterhouse-Five

Nonviolence is the answer to the crucial political
and moral questions of our time; the need for man
to overcome oppression and violence without
resorting to oppression and violence.
Man must evolve for all human conflict a method
which rejects revenge, aggression and retaliation.
The foundation of such a method is love.

Martin Luther King Jr., Speech accepting the Nobel Peace Prize

When elephants fight it is the grass that suffers.

Anonymous, African proverb

Science and Progress

There are in fact two things, science and opinion; the former begets knowledge, the latter ignorance.

Hippocrates, Law

Happy the man who could search out the causes of things.

Virgil, Georgics

[Human reason] freed men's minds from wondering at portents by wresting from Jupiter his bolts and power of thunder, and ascribing to the winds the noise and to the clouds the flame.

Marcus Manilius, Astronomica

Facts which at first seem improbable will, even on scant explanation, drop the cloak which has hidden them and stand forth in naked and simple beauty.

Galileo Galilei, Dialogues Concerning Two New Sciences

The truth is, the science of Nature has been already too long made only a work of the brain and the fancy: It is now high time that it should return to the plainness and soundness of observations on material and obvious things.

Robert Hooke, Micrographia

Facts are stubborn things.

Alain René Lesage, Gil Blas

Give me the political economist, the sanitary reformer, the engineer; and take your saints and virgins, relics and miracles. The spinning-jenny and the railroad, Cunard's liners and the electric telegraph, are to me . . . signs that we are, on some points at least, in harmony with the universe.

Charles Kingsley, Yeast

Progress, therefore, is not an accident, but a necessity. . . . It is a part of nature.

Herbert Spencer, Social Statics

Life is a wave, which in no two consecutive moments of its existence is composed of the same particles.

John Tyndall, Fragments of Science

Whoever, in the pursuit of science, seeks after immediate practical utility, may generally rest assured that he will seek in vain. All that science can achieve is a perfect knowledge and a perfect understanding of the action of natural and moral forces.

Hermann Ludwig Ferdinand von Helmholtz,
Academic discourse, Heidelberg

The great tragedy of Science — the slaying of a
beautiful hypothesis by an ugly fact.

T. H. Huxley, Biogenesis and Abiogenesis

Physics is experience, arranged in economical order.

Ernst Mach, The Economical Nature of Physical Inquiry

Remember, then, that it [science] is the guide of action; that
the truth which it arrives at is not that which we can ideally
contemplate without error, but that which we may act
upon without fear; and you cannot fail to see that
scientific thought is not an accompaniment or condition
of human progress, but human progress itself.

William Kingdon Clifford, Aims and Instruments of Scientific Thought

Every great advance in science has issued from
a new audacity of imagination.

John Dewey, The Quest for Certainty

The science of pure mathematics, in its modern
developments, may claim to be the most
original creation of the human spirit.

Alfred North Whitehead, Science and the Modern World

The most beautiful thing we can experience is the
mysterious. It is the source of all true art and science.

Albert Einstein, What I Believe

Art upsets, science reassures.

Georges Braque, Pensées sur l'Art

One of the things which distinguishes ours from all earlier
generations is this, that we have seen our atoms.

Karl Kelchner Darrow, The Renaissance of Physics

There is only one proved method of assisting the
advancement of pure science — that of picking men
of genius, backing them heavily, and leaving
them to direct themselves.

James Bryant Conant, Letter to the New York Times

Discovery consists of seeing what everybody has seen
and thinking what nobody has thought.

Albert Szent-Györgyi von Nagyrapolt,
From I. J. Good (ed.), The Scientist Speculates

Technology . . . the knack of so arranging
the world that we don't have to experience it.

Max Frisch, Homo Faber

The scientist values research by the size of its contribution
to that huge, logically articulated structure of ideas
which is already, though not yet half built, the
most glorious accomplishment of mankind.

Sir Peter Brian Medawar, The Art of the Soluble

If we do discover a complete [unified] theory [of the
universe], it should in time be understandable in
broad principle by everyone, not just a few scientists.
Then we shall all, philosophers, scientists, and just
ordinary people, be able to take part in the
discussion of the question of why it is that we and
the universe exist. If we find the answer to that,
it would be the ultimate triumph of human reason —
for then we should know the mind of God.

Stephen Hawking, A Brief History of Time

Strength and Courage

Let the counsel of thine own heart stand.
*The Bible, The Apocrypha, The Wisdom of Jesus
the Son of Sirach, or Ecclesiasticus*

Resist not evil: but whosoever shall smite thee on
thy right cheek, turn to him the other also.
The Bible, Matthew

One finds many companions for food and drink, but in a
serious business a man's companions are very few.
Theognis, Elegies

Great deeds are usually wrought at great risks.
Herodotus, Histories

Fortune favors the brave.
Virgil, Aeneid

The man who is tenacious of purpose in a rightful cause
is not shaken from his firm resolve by the frenzy of
his fellow citizens clamoring for what is wrong,
or by the tyrant's threatening countenance.

Horace, Odes

What though strength fails? Boldness is certain to
win praise. In mighty enterprises, it is enough to
have had the determination.

Sextus Propertius, Elegies

Those who'll play with cats must expect to be scratched.

Miguel de Cervantes, Don Quixote

The better part of valor is discretion.

William Shakespeare, King Henry the Fourth, Part I

To do a great right, do a little wrong.

William Shakespeare, The Merchant of Venice

When our actions do not,
Our fears do make us traitors.

William Shakespeare, Macbeth

Great actions are not always true sons
Of great and mighty resolutions.
Samuel Butler, Hudibras

The greatest weakness of all weaknesses is to
fear too much to appear weak.
Jacques Bénigne Bossuet, Politique Tirée de l'Écriture Sainte

Tender-handed stroke a nettle,
And it stings you for your pains;
Grasp it like a man of mettle,
And it soft as silk remains.
Aaron Hill, Verses Written on a Window in Scotland

The first step is the hardest.
Marie de Vichy-Chamrond, Marquise du Deffand, Letter to d'Alembert

Without justice, courage is weak.
Benjamin Franklin, Poor Richard's Almanac

They that can give up essential liberty to obtain a little
temporary safety deserve neither liberty nor safety.
Benjamin Franklin, Historical Review of Pennsylvania

Only the brave know how to forgive. . . .
A coward never forgave; it is not in his nature.

Laurence Sterne, Sermons

Great souls suffer in silence.

Johann Friedrich von Schiller, Don Carlos

One man with courage makes a majority.

Andrew Jackson, Attributed

Who would be free themselves must strike the blow.

George Noel Gordon, Lord Byron, Childe Harold's Pilgrimage

To believe your own thought, to believe that what
is true for you in your private heart is true
for all men — that is genius.

Ralph Waldo Emerson, Essays

Speak the affirmative; emphasize your choice
by utter ignoring of all that you reject.

Ralph Waldo Emerson, Lectures and Biographical Sketches

Whatever crushes individuality is despotism,
by whatever name it may be called.

John Stuart Mill, On Liberty

Bravery never goes out of fashion.

William Makepeace Thackeray, The Four Georges

To dry one's eyes and laugh at a fall,
And baffled, get up and begin again.

Robert Browning, Life in a Love

You'll find us rough, sir, but you'll find us ready.

Charles Dickens, David Copperfield

If a man does not keep pace with his companions, perhaps
it is because he hears a different drummer. Let him step to
the music which he hears, however measured or far away.

Henry David Thoreau, Walden

And I honor the man who is willing to sink
Half his present repute for the freedom to think,
And, when he has thought, be his cause strong or weak,
Will risk t' other half for the freedom to speak.

James Russell Lowell, A Fable for Critics

Cautious, careful people, always casting about to preserve
their reputation and social standing, never can bring about
a reform. Those who are really in earnest must be willing
to be anything or nothing in the world's estimation.

Susan B. Anthony, On the campaign for divorce law reform

I started with this idea in my head, "There's two
things I've got a right to . . . death or liberty."
Harriet Tubman, To her biographer Sarah H. Bradford

Be neither saint- nor sophist-led, but be a man!
Matthew Arnold, Empedocles on Etna

Choose equality.
Matthew Arnold, Mixed Essays

The strongest man in the world is
he who stands most alone.
Henrik Ibsen, An Enemy of the People

Pray for the dead and fight like hell for the living!
Mother Jones, Autobiography

Heroism, the Caucasian mountaineers say,
is endurance for one moment more.
George Kennan, Letter to Henry Munroe Rogers

Far better it is to dare mighty things, to win glorious
triumphs, even though checkered by failure, than
to take rank with those poor spirits who neither
enjoy much nor suffer much, because they live in
the gray twilight that knows not victory nor defeat.

Theodore Roosevelt, Speech before the Hamilton Club, Chicago

In life, as in a football game, the principle to follow is:
Hit the line hard.

Theodore Roosevelt, The Strenuous Life: Essays and Addresses

The value of a sentiment is the amount of
sacrifice you are prepared to make for it.

John Galsworthy, Windows

The cost of liberty is less than the price of repression.

William Edward Burghardt Du Bois, John Brown

Death and sorrow will be the companions of our journey;
hardship our garment; constancy and valor our only
shield. We must be united, we must be undaunted,
we must be inflexible.

Sir Winston Spencer Churchill, Report on the war, House of Commons

You gain strength, courage and confidence by every
experience in which you really stop to look fear in the face.
You are able to say to yourself, "I lived through this horror.
I can take the next thing that comes along." . . . You
must do the thing you think you cannot do.

Eleanor Roosevelt, You Learn by Living

The strong lean upon death as on a rock.

Robinson Jeffers, Gale in April

We know too much, and are convinced of too little. Our
literature is a substitute for religion, and so is our religion.

T. S. Eliot, A Dialogue on Dramatic Poetry

Show me a good and gracious loser
and I'll show you a failure.

Knute Rockne, Remark to Wisconsin basketball coach Walter Meanwell

He is immortal, not because he alone among creatures has
an inexhaustible voice, but because he has a soul, a spirit
capable of compassion and sacrifice and endurance.

William Faulkner, Speech upon receiving the Nobel Prize

Grace under pressure.

Ernest Hemingway, Definition of "guts"

I cannot and will not cut my conscience
to fit this year's fashions.

Lillian Hellman, Letter to the House Committee on Un-American Activities

There comes a time in a man's life when to get where
he has to go — if there are no doors or
windows — he walks through a wall.

Bernard Malamud, Rembrandt's Hat

Let us never negotiate out of fear, but let
us never fear to negotiate.

John Fitzgerald Kennedy, Inaugural address

When you come to a fork in the road, take it.

Yogi Berra, Attributed

History, despite its wrenching pain,
Cannot be unlived, but if faced
With courage, need not be lived again.

Maya Angelou, On the Pulse of Morning

Whoever is happy will make others happy too. He who
has courage and faith will never perish in misery!

Anne Frank, Anne Frank: The Diary of a Young Girl

If a man hasn't discovered something that he will die for, he isn't fit to live.

Martin Luther King Jr., Speech in Detroit

I refuse to accept the idea that the "isness" of man's present nature makes him morally incapable of reaching up for the "oughtness" that forever confronts him.

Martin Luther King Jr., Speech accepting the Nobel Peace Prize

If I have to, I can do anything.
I am strong, I am invincible, I am woman.

Helen Reddy, I Am Woman

Float like a butterfly, sting like a bee.

Muhammad Ali, Boxing credo

Our hearts are broken, but they continue to beat, and the spirit of our City has never been stronger.

Rudolph W. Giuliani, One Nation: America Remembers September 11, 2001

Climb high
Climb far
Your goal the sky
Your aim the star.

Anonymous, Inscription on Hopkins Memorial Steps, Williams College, Williamstown, Massachusetts

Time

Let us eat and drink; for tomorrow we shall die.

The Bible, The Book of the Prophet Isaiah

Time eases all things.

Sophocles, Oedipus Rex

Rash indeed is he who reckons on the morrow, or haply on days beyond it; for tomorrow is not, until today is past.

Sophocles, Trachiniae

Time is the most valuable thing a man can spend.

Theophrastus, From Diogenes Laertius, Lives of Eminent Philosophers

Time removes distress.

Terence, Heauton Timoroumenos

The ring on the finger becomes thin beneath by wearing, the fall of dripping water hollows the stone.

Lucretius, De Rerum Natura

Seize the day, put no trust in the morrow!

Horace, Odes

Time the devourer of all things.

Ovid, Metamorphoses

Time discovers truth.

Lucius Annaeus Seneca, Moral Essays

Pythagoras, when he was asked what time was,
answered that it was the soul of this world.

Plutarch, Morals

How much time he gains who does not look to see what
his neighbor says or does or thinks, but only at what
he does himself, to make it just and holy.

Marcus Aurelius Antoninus, Meditations

Time is a sort of river of passing events, and strong is
its current; no sooner is a thing brought to sight
than it is swept by and another takes its place,
and this too will be swept away.

Marcus Aurelius Antoninus, Meditations

For to lose time is most displeasing
to him who knows most.
Dante Alighieri, The Divine Comedy

For tyme ylost may nought recovered be.
Geoffrey Chaucer, Troilus and Criseyde

For thogh we slepe, or wake, or rome, or ryde,
Ay fleeth the tyme, it nyl no man abyde.
Geoffrey Chaucer, The Canterbury Tales

Time takes all and gives all.
Giordano Bruno, The Candle Bearer

Better three hours too soon than a minute too late.
William Shakespeare, The Merry Wives of Windsor

What's past and what's to come is strew'd with husks
And formless ruin of oblivion.
William Shakespeare, Troilus and Cressida

Come what come may,
Time and the hour runs through the roughest day.
William Shakespeare, Macbeth

Like as the waves make towards the pebbled shore,
So do our minutes hasten to their end.

William Shakespeare, Sonnet 60

That old bald cheater, Time.

Ben Jonson, The Poetaster

Gather ye rosebuds while ye may,
Old Time is still a-flying,
And this same flower that smiles today
Tomorrow will be dying.

Robert Herrick, Hesperides

The never-ending flight
Of future days.

John Milton, Paradise Lost

On the wings of Time grief flies away.

Jean de La Fontaine, Fables

No time like the present.

Mary de la Rivière Manley, The Lost Lover

Procrastination is the thief of time.

Edward Young, Night Thoughts

Dost thou love life? Then do not squander time;
for that's the stuff life is made of.

Benjamin Franklin, Poor Richard's Almanac

Remember that time is money.

Benjamin Franklin, Advice to a Young Tradesman

One crowded hour of glorious life
Is worth an age without a name.

Thomas Osbert Mordaunt, Verses Written During the War

Delay is preferable to error.

Thomas Jefferson, Letter to George Washington

Time is man's angel.

Johann Friedrich von Schiller, The Death of Wallenstein

If you keep a thing seven years, you are
sure to find a use for it.

Sir Walter Scott, Woodstock

Do not shorten the morning by getting up late; look upon it
as the quintessence of life, as to a certain extent sacred.

Arthur Schopenhauer, Counsels and Maxims

This time, like all times, is a very good one,
if we but know what to do with it.

Ralph Waldo Emerson, The American Scholar

You cannot fight against the future. Time is on our side.

William Ewart Gladstone, Speech on the Reform Bill

As if you could kill time without injuring eternity.

Henry David Thoreau, Walden

Time is but the stream I go a-fishing in.

Henry David Thoreau, Walden

Things always seem fairer when we look back at them,
and it is out of that inaccessible tower of the past
that Longing leans and beckons.

James Russell Lowell, Literary Essays

The strongest of all warriors are these two —
Time and Patience.

Leo Nikolaevich Tolstoi, War and Peace

Let anyone try, I will not say to arrest, but to notice or attend to, the present moment of time. One of the most baffling experiences occurs. Where is it, this present? It has melted in our grasp, fled ere we could touch it, gone in the instant of becoming.

William James, The Principles of Psychology

Everything happens to everybody sooner or later if there is time enough.

George Bernard Shaw, Back to Methuselah

Those who cannot remember the past are condemned to repeat it.

George Santayana, The Life of Reason

The past is but the beginning of a beginning, and all that is and has been is but the twilight of the dawn.

H. G. Wells, The Discovery of the Future

What is this life if, full of care, We have no time to stand and stare?

W. H. Davies, Leisure

The time which we have at our disposal every day is elastic; the passions that we feel expand it, those that we inspire contract it; and habit fills up what remains.

Marcel Proust, Remembrance of Things Past

Poor Jim Jay
Got stuck fast
In Yesterday.

Walter de la Mare, Jim Jay

Now this is not the end. It is not even the beginning of the
end. But it is, perhaps, the end of the beginning.

*Sir Winston Spencer Churchill, Speech at the
Lord Mayor's Day Luncheon, London*

We can only pay our debt to the past by
putting the future in debt to ourselves.

*John Buchan, Lord Tweedsmuir, Address to the people of Canada,
on the coronation of George VI*

Hold fast the time! Guard it, watch over it, every hour, every
minute! Unregarded it slips away, like a lizard, smooth,
slippery, faithless, a pixy wife. Hold every moment sacred.
Give each clarity and meaning, each the weight of thine
awareness, each its true and due fulfillment.

Thomas Mann, The Beloved Returns

Time present and time past
Are both perhaps present in time future,
And time future contained in time past.

T. S. Eliot, Four Quartets

Only through time time is conquered.
T. S. Eliot, Four Quartets

Time the destroyer is time the preserver.
T. S. Eliot, Four Quartets

You're only here for a short visit. Don't hurry. Don't worry.
And be sure to smell the flowers along the way.
Walter C. Hagen, The Walter Hagen Story

The past is a foreign country;
they do things differently there.
L. P. Hartley, The Go-Between

In a real dark night of the soul it is always
three o'clock in the morning.
F. Scott Fitzgerald, The Crack-up

The Future . . . something which everyone reaches
at the rate of sixty minutes an hour,
whatever he does, whoever he is.
C. S. Lewis, The Screwtape Letters

Time is the least thing we have of.
Ernest Hemingway, From The New Yorker profile by Lillian Ross

Death and taxes and childbirth! There's never any
convenient time for any of them.

Margaret Mitchell, Gone With the Wind

Time wounds all heels.

Jane Ace, From Goodman Ace,
The Fine Art of Hypochondria; or, How Are You?

Work expands so as to fill the time
available for its completion.

C. Northcote Parkinson, Parkinson's Law

We haven't the time to take our time.

Eugène Ionesco, Exit the King (Le Roi Se Meurt)

Time is the school in which we learn,
Time is the fire in which we burn.

Delmore Schwartz, For Rhoda

Always that same old story —
Father Time and Mother Earth,
A marriage on the rocks.

James Merrill, The Broken Home

The earth's about five million years old, at least.
Who can afford to live in the past?

Harold Pinter, The Homecoming

Time is of the essence.

Anonymous, Saying

Time is a river without banks.

Anonymous, Saying

Truth

Truth is great and its effectiveness endures.

Ptahhotpe, The Maxims of Ptahhotpe

Great is Truth, and mighty above all things.

The Bible, The Apocrypha, I Esdras

Beware of false prophets, which come to you in sheep's clothing, but inwardly they are ravening wolves.

The Bible, Matthew

The truth shall make you free.

The Bible, The Gospel According to Saint John

Truths kindle light for truths.

Lucretius, De Rerum Natura

Truth persuades by teaching, but does not teach by persuading.

Tertullian, Adversus Valentinianos

In wine is truth.

Anonymous, Latin proverb

I believe that in the end the truth will conquer.

John Wycliffe, To the Duke of Lancaster

Superstition, idolatry, and hypocrisy have ample wages, but truth goes a-begging.

Martin Luther, Table Talk

Speak the truth and shame the Devil.

François Rabelais, Gargantua and Pantagruel

Honesty's the best policy.

Miguel de Cervantes, Don Quixote

Be so true to thyself, as thou be not false to others.

Francis Bacon, Essays

Truth hath a quiet breast.

William Shakespeare, King Richard the Second

This above all: to thine own self be true,
And it must follow, as the night the day,
Thou canst not then be false to any man.
William Shakespeare, Hamlet

My words fly up, my thoughts remain below:
Words without thoughts never to heaven go.
William Shakespeare, Hamlet

Truth is truth
To the end of reckoning.
William Shakespeare, Measure for Measure

To show an unfelt sorrow is an office
Which the false man does easy.
William Shakespeare, Macbeth

The dignity of truth is lost with much protesting.
Ben Jonson, Catiline's Conspiracy

The first precept was never to accept a thing as true until I
knew it as such without a single doubt.
René Descartes, Le Discours de la Méthode

A few honest men are better than numbers.
Oliver Cromwell, Letter to Sir W. Spring

We know the truth, not only by
the reason, but by the heart.

Blaise Pascal, Pensées

It is one thing to show a man that he is in an error, and
another to put him in possession of truth.

John Locke, Essay Concerning Human Understanding

Nothing but truth is lovely, nothing fair.

Nicolas Boileau-Despréaux, Epistle 9

Truth often suffers more by the heat of its defenders than
from the arguments of its opposers.

William Penn, Some Fruits of Solitude

When we risk no contradiction,
It prompts the tongue to deal in fiction.

John Gay, Fables

Love truth, but pardon error.

Voltaire, Sept Discours en Vers sur l'Homme

He who permits himself to tell a lie once, finds it much
easier to do it a second and third time, till at length it
becomes habitual; he tells lies without attending to it,
and truths without the world's believing him. This
falsehood of the tongue leads to that of the heart,
and in time depraves all its good dispositions.

Thomas Jefferson, Letter to Peter Carr

We are not afraid to follow truth wherever it
may lead, nor to tolerate any error so long
as reason is left free to combat it.

Thomas Jefferson, Letter to William Roscoe

Nothing is more damaging to a new truth than an old error.

Johann Wolfgang von Goethe, Proverbs in Prose

Truth can never be told so as to be understood,
and not be believ'd.

William Blake, The Marriage of Heaven and Hell

A truth that's told with bad intent
Beats all the lies you can invent.

William Blake, Poems from the Pickering Manuscript

Oh, what a tangled web we weave,
When first we practice to deceive!

Sir Walter Scott, Marmion

Sin has many tools, but a lie is the
handle which fits them all.

Oliver Wendell Holmes, The Autocrat of the Breakfast-Table

Truth is generally the best vindication against slander.

Abraham Lincoln, Letter to Secretary Stanton

Truth is one forever absolute, but opinion is truth
filtered through the moods, the blood,
the disposition of the spectator.

Wendell Phillips, Idols

So absolutely good is truth,
truth never hurts
The teller.

Robert Browning, Fifine at the Fair

It takes two to speak the truth —
one to speak, and another to hear.

Henry David Thoreau, A Week on the Concord and Merrimack Rivers

Rather than love, than money, than fame, give me truth.

Henry David Thoreau, Walden

The essence of lying is in deception, not in words.

John Ruskin, Modern Painters

Truth sits upon the lips of dying men.
Matthew Arnold, Sohrab and Rustum

Every man is fully satisfied that there is such a thing
as truth, or he would not ask any question.
Charles Sanders Peirce, Collected Papers

Certitude is not the test of certainty.
Oliver Wendell Holmes Jr., Natural Law

No one is such a liar as the indignant man.
Friedrich Wilhelm Nietzsche, Beyond Good and Evil

When will women begin to have the first glimmer that
above all other loyalties is the loyalty to Truth, i.e., to
yourself, that husband, children, friends
and country are as nothing to that?
Alice James, Diary

All great truths begin as blasphemies.
George Bernard Shaw, Annajanska

When you have eliminated the impossible, whatever
remains, however improbable, must be the truth.
Sir Arthur Conan Doyle, The Sign of Four

There are no whole truths; all truths are half-truths. It is
trying to treat them as whole truths that plays the devil.
Alfred North Whitehead, Dialogues of Alfred North Whitehead

Nonviolence and truth (Satya) are inseparable and presup-
pose one another. There is no god higher than truth.
Mahatma Gandhi, True Patriotism

Truth has no special time of its own.
Its hour is now — always.
Albert Schweitzer, Out of My Life and Thought

Only when we realize that there is no eternal,
unchanging truth or absolute truth can we arouse
in ourselves a sense of intellectual responsibility.
Hu Shih, La Jeunesse Nouvelle

If ever I said, in grief or pride,
I tired of honest things, I lied.
Edna St. Vincent Millay, The Goose Girl

Marvelous Truth, confront us
at every turn,
in every guise.
Denise Levertov, Matins

Virtue and Vice

But of the tree of the knowledge of good and evil,
thou shalt not eat of it: for in the day that thou
eatest thereof thou shalt surely die.

The Bible, The First Book of Moses, Called Genesis

Keep thy tongue from evil,
and thy lips from speaking guile.
Depart from evil, and do good;
seek peace, and pursue it.

The Bible, The Book of Psalms

Woe unto them that call evil good, and good evil.

The Bible, The Book of the Prophet Isaiah

They be blind leaders of the blind. And if the blind
lead the blind, both shall fall into the ditch.

The Bible, Matthew

Watch and pray, that ye enter not into temptation:
the spirit indeed is willing, but the flesh is weak.

The Bible, Matthew

Be not overcome of evil, but overcome evil with good.
The Bible, The Epistle of Paul the Apostle to the Romans

Blessed is the man that endureth temptation: for when
he is tried, he shall receive the crown of life.
The Bible, The General Epistle of James

He harms himself who does harm to another,
and the evil plan is most harmful to the planner.
Hesiod, Works and Days

I have three treasures. Guard and keep them:
The first is deep love,
The second is frugality,
And the third is not to dare to be ahead of the world.
Because of deep love, one is courageous.
Because of frugality, one is generous.
Because of not daring to be ahead of the world, one be-
comes the leader of the world.
Lao-tzu, The Way of Lao-tzu

Virtue is not left to stand alone. He who practices it will
have neighbors.
Confucius, Analects

The man of virtue makes the difficulty to be overcome his
first business, and success only a subsequent consideration.

Confucius, Analects

Is virtue a thing remote? I wish to be virtuous,
and lo! virtue is at hand.

Confucius, Analects

Never has a man who has bent himself
been able to make others straight.

Mencius, Works

To flee vice is the beginning of virtue, and to have
got rid of folly is the beginning of wisdom.

Horace, Epistles

A liar should have a good memory.

Quintilian, De Institutione Oratoria

Virtue extends our days: he lives two lives
who relives his past with pleasure.

Martial, Epigrams

The very spring and root of honesty
and virtue lie in good education.

Plutarch, Morals

A wrongdoer is often a man who has left some thing
undone, not always one who has done something.

Marcus Aurelius Antoninus, Meditations

Whoever destroys a single life is as guilty as though
he had destroyed the entire world; and whoever
rescues a single life earns as much merit as
though he had rescued the entire world.

Talmud

Envy slays itself by its own arrows.

Anonymous, The Greek Anthology

The easy, gentle, and sloping path . . . is not the path of
true virtue. It demands a rough and thorny road.

Michel Eyquem de Montaigne, Essays

I find that the best goodness I have
has some tincture of vice.

Michel Eyquem de Montaigne, Essays

Can we ever have too much of a good thing?

Miguel de Cervantes, Don Quixote

He lives in fame that died in virtue's cause.

William Shakespeare, Titus Andronicus

Virtue itself turns vice, being misapplied;
And vice sometime's by action dignified.
William Shakespeare, Romeo and Juliet

There is no vice so simple but assumes
Some mark of virtue on his outward parts.
William Shakespeare, The Merchant of Venice

Assume a virtue, if you have it not.
William Shakespeare, Hamlet

Good company and good discourse
are the very sinews of virtue.
Izaak Walton, The Compleat Angler

I cannot praise a fugitive and cloistered virtue, unexercised
and unbreathed, that never sallies out and sees her
adversary, but slinks out of the race, where that immortal
garland is to be run for, not without dust and heat.
John Milton, Areopagitica

If we had no faults of our own, we would not take
so much pleasure in noticing those of others.
François, Duc de La Rochefoucauld, Reflections

Hypocrisy is the homage that vice pays to virtue.
François, Duc de La Rochefoucauld, Reflections

Although I am a pious man, I am not the less a man.
Molière, Tartuffe

If everyone were clothed with integrity, if every heart were
just, frank, kindly, the other virtues would be well-nigh
useless, since their chief purpose is to make us bear
with patience the injustice of our fellows.
Molière, Le Misanthrope

Thanks be to God, since my leaving drinking of wine,
I do find myself much better, and do mind my
business better, and do spend less money,
and less time lost in idle company.
Samuel Pepys, Diary

Popularity is a crime from the moment it is sought; it is only
a virtue where men have it whether they will or no.
George Savile, Marquess of Halifax,
Political, Moral, and Miscellaneous Reflections

Among all the diseases of the mind there is not one more
epidemical or more pernicious than the love of flattery.
Sir Richard Steele, The Spectator

For Satan finds some mischief still
For idle hands to do.
Isaac Watts, Divine Songs

But when to mischief mortals bend their will,
How soon they find fit instruments of ill!
Alexander Pope, The Rape of the Lock

Virtue is not always amiable.
John Adams, Diary

When we are planning for posterity, we ought
to remember that virtue is not hereditary.
Thomas Paine, Common Sense

A thing moderately good is not so good as it ought to be.
Moderation in temper is always a virtue; but moderation
in principle is always a vice.
Thomas Paine, The Rights of Man

No man chooses evil because it is evil; he only mistakes
it for happiness, the good he seeks.
Mary Wollstonecraft, A Vindication of the Rights of Men

Virtue can only flourish amongst equals.
Mary Wollstonecraft, A Vindication of the Rights of Men

Character is higher than intellect.
Ralph Waldo Emerson, The American Scholar

More people are flattered into virtue
than bullied out of vice.
Robert Smith Surtees, The Analysis of the Hunting Field

There is no odor so bad as that which
arises from goodness tainted.
Henry David Thoreau, Walden

Bad work follers ye ez long's ye live.
James Russell Lowell, The Biglow Papers

It is not enough to do good; one must do it the right way.
John, Viscount Morley of Blackburn, Rousseau

We are spinning our own fates, good or evil, and never to
be undone. Every smallest stroke of virtue or of vice
leaves its never so little scar . . . Nothing we ever
do is, in strict scientific literalness, wiped out.
William James, The Principles of Psychology

An act has no ethical quality whatever unless it be
chosen out of several all equally possible.
William James, The Principles of Psychology

The only way to get rid of a temptation is to yield to it.
Oscar Wilde, The Picture of Dorian Gray

Virtue consists, not in abstaining from vice,
but in not desiring it.
George Bernard Shaw, Man and Superman

Necessary, forever necessary, to burn out false shames
and smelt the heaviest ore of the body into purity.
D. H. Lawrence, Lady Chatterley's Lover

I know only that what is moral is what you feel good after
and what is immoral is what you feel bad after.
Ernest Hemingway, Death in the Afternoon

Hear no evil, see no evil, speak no evil.
Anonymous, Legend related to the "Three Wise Monkeys"

Wealth and Poverty

Do not set your heart on wealth
Do not strain to seek increases,
What you have, let it suffice you.
If riches come to you by theft,
They will not stay the night with you. . . .
They made themselves wings like geese,
And flew away to the sky.

Amenemope, The Instruction of Amenemope

He that trusteth in his riches shall fall.

The Bible, The Proverbs

Wealth maketh many friends.

The Bible, The Proverbs

The borrower is servant to the lender.

The Bible, The Proverbs

A feast is made for laughter, and wine maketh merry:
but money answereth all things.

The Bible, Ecclesiastes; or, The Preacher

In the day of prosperity there is a forgetfulness of affliction:
and in the day of affliction there is no more
remembrance of prosperity.

*The Bible, The Apocrypha, The Wisdom of Jesus
the Son of Sirach, or Ecclesiasticus*

It is easier for a camel to go through the eye of a needle,
than for a rich man to enter into the kingdom of God.

The Bible, Matthew

The love of money is the root of all evil.

The Bible, The First Epistle of Paul the Apostle to Timothy

There is no calamity greater than lavish desires.
There is no greater guilt than discontentment.
And there is no greater disaster than greed.

Lao-tzu, The Way of Lao-tzu

Money: There's nothing in the world
so demoralizing as money.

Sophocles, Antigone

Wisdom outweighs any wealth.

Sophocles, Antigone

He has not acquired a fortune;
the fortune has acquired him.

Bion, From Diogenes Laertius, Lives of Eminent Philosophers

A farm is like a man — however great the income,
if there is extravagance but little is left.

Cato the Elder, On Agriculture

I have everything, yet have nothing; and although I possess
nothing, still of nothing am I in want.

Terence, Eunuchus

In truth, prosperity tries the souls even of the wise.

Sallust, The War with Catiline

Whoever cultivates the golden mean avoids both the
poverty of a hovel and the envy of a palace.

Horace, Odes

He is not poor who has enough of things to use.
If it is well with your belly, chest and feet, the
wealth of kings can give you nothing more.

Horace, Epistles

Whatever you can lose, you should reckon of no account.

Publilius Syrus, Maxim

An object in possession seldom retains the
same charm that it had in pursuit.

Pliny the Younger, Letters

The loss of wealth is loss of dirt,
As sages in all times assert;
The happy man's without a shirt.

John Heywood, Be Merry Friends

Beggars should be no choosers.

John Heywood, Proverbs

A little in one's own pocket is better than much in
another man's purse. 'Tis good to keep a
nest egg. Every little makes a mickle.

Miguel de Cervantes, Don Quixote

Money is like muck, not good except it be spread.

Francis Bacon, Essays

Fortune is like the market, where many times,
if you can stay a little, the price will fall.

Francis Bacon, Essays

Excess of wealth is cause of covetousness.

Christopher Marlowe, The Jew of Malta

Having nothing, nothing can he lose.
William Shakespeare, King Henry the Sixth, Part III

They are as sick that surfeit with too much as they that
starve with nothing.
William Shakespeare, The Merchant of Venice

I can get no remedy against this consumption of the purse:
borrowing only lingers and lingers it out,
but the disease is incurable.
William Shakespeare, King Henry the Fourth, Part II

Neither a borrower, nor a lender be;
For loan oft loses both itself and friend,
And borrowing dulls the edge of husbandry.
William Shakespeare, Hamlet

Penny wise, pound foolish.
Robert Burton, The Anatomy of Melancholy

To give aid to every poor man is far beyond the reach
and power of every man. . . . Care of the poor is
incumbent on society as a whole.
Benedict Spinoza, Ethics

Money speaks sense in a language all nations understand.

Aphra Behn, The Rover

It is a reproach to religion and government to
suffer so much poverty and excess.

William Penn, Some Fruits of Solitude

Let all the learned say what they can,
'Tis ready money makes the man.

William Somerville, Ready Money

Necessity never made a good bargain.

Benjamin Franklin, Poor Richard's Almanac

It is better to live rich, than to die rich.

Samuel Johnson, From Boswell, Life of Johnson

Whatever you have, spend less.

Samuel Johnson, From Boswell, Life of Johnson

Where wealth and freedom reign contentment fails,
And honor sinks where commerce long prevails.

Oliver Goldsmith, The Traveller

Never buy what you do not want, because it is cheap;
it will be dear to you.

*Thomas Jefferson, A Decalogue of Canons for Observation
in Practical Life*

Put not your trust in money, but put your money in trust.

Oliver Wendell Holmes, The Autocrat of the Breakfast-Table

Money and goods are certainly the best of references.

Charles Dickens, Our Mutual Friend

That man is the richest whose pleasures are the cheapest.

Henry David Thoreau, Journal

Poverty iz the stepmother ov genius.

Josh Billings, His Sayings

There is no wealth but life.

John Ruskin, Unto This Last

Every increased possession loads us with a new weariness.

John Ruskin, The Eagle's Nest

So long as all the increased wealth which modern progress
brings goes but to build up great fortunes, to increase
luxury and make sharper the contrast between the
House of Have and the House of Want, progress
is not real and cannot be permanent.

Henry George, Progress and Poverty

If a man is wise, he gets rich, an' if he gets rich,
he gets foolish, or his wife does.
That's what keeps the money movin' around.

Finley Peter Dunne, Observations by Mr. Dooley

When a fellow says it hain't the money but the
principle o' the thing, it's th' money.

Frank McKinney "Kin" Hubbard, Hoss Sense and Nonsense

Poverty keeps together more homes than it breaks up.

Saki, The Chronicles of Clovis

Economic distress will teach men, if anything can, that
realities are less dangerous than fancies, that fact-finding
is more effective than fault-finding.

Carl Becker, Progress and Power

Always try to rub up against money, for if you rub up
against money long enough, some of it may rub off on you.

Damon Runyon, Guys and Dolls

In revolutionary times the rich are always
the people who are most afraid.

Gerald White Johnson, American Freedom and the Press

Let me tell you about the very rich. They are different from
you and me. They possess and enjoy early, and it does
something to them, makes them soft where we are hard,
and cynical where we are trustful.

F. Scott Fitzgerald, The Rich Boy

The rich were dull and they drank too much. . . . He
remembered poor Julian and his romantic awe of them and
how he had started a story once that began, "The very rich
are different from you and me." And how someone had
said to Julian, Yes, they have more money.

Ernest Hemingway, The Fifth Column and The First Forty-Nine Stories

Boredom is the keynote of poverty . . . for where
there is no money there is no change of any kind,
not of scene or of routine.

Moss Hart, Act One

Wealth is not without its advantages and the case to
the contrary, although it has often been made,
has never proved widely persuasive.

John Kenneth Galbraith, The Affluent Society

Wisdom and Knowledge

With the ancient is wisdom; and in length
of days understanding.

The Bible, The Book of Job

The price of wisdom is above rubies.

The Bible, The Book of Job

Wisdom is the principal thing; therefore get wisdom:
and with all thy getting get understanding.

The Bible, The Proverbs

A wise son maketh a glad father: but a foolish son
is the heaviness of his mother.

The Bible, The Proverbs

He that hath knowledge spareth his words: and a man of
understanding is of an excellent spirit.
Even a fool, when he holdeth his peace, is counted wise.

The Bible, The Proverbs

A wise man is strong; yea, a man of
knowledge increaseth strength.

The Bible, The Proverbs

In much wisdom is much grief: and he that
increaseth knowledge increaseth sorrow.

The Bible, Ecclesiastes; or, The Preacher

Wisdom excelleth folly, as far as light excelleth darkness.

The Bible, Ecclesiastes; or, The Preacher

Wisdom exalteth her children, and
layeth hold of them that seek her.
He that loveth her loveth life.

*The Bible, The Apocrypha, The Wisdom of Jesus
the Son of Sirach, or Ecclesiasticus*

A foolish man, which built his house upon the sand.

The Bible, Matthew

The fox knows many things, but the
hedgehog knows one great thing.

Archilochus, Fragment

Know thyself.

The Seven Sages, Inscription at the Delphic Oracle

He who knows others is wise;
He who knows himself is enlightened.

Lao-tzu, The Way of Lao-tzu

He who knows does not speak.
He who speaks does not know.

Lao-tzu, The Way of Lao-tzu

To know that you do not know is the best.
To pretend to know when you do not know is a disease.

Lao-tzu, The Way of Lao-tzu

It takes a wise man to recognize a wise man.

Xenophanes, From Diogenes Laertius, Lives of Eminent Philosophers

If a man withdraws his mind from the love of beauty, and
applies it as sincerely to the love of the virtuous; if, in serving his parents, he can exert his utmost strength; if, in serving his prince, he can devote his life; if, in his intercourse
with his friends, his words are sincere — although men say
that he has not learned, I will certainly say that he has.

Confucius, Analects

When you know a thing, to hold that you know it; and
when you do not know a thing, to allow that you
do not know it — this is knowledge.

Confucius, Analects

In this world second thoughts, it seems, are best.

Euripides, Hippolytus

The wise learn many things from their enemies.

Aristophanes, Birds

Wise men profit more from fools than fools from wise men;
for the wise men shun the mistakes of fools, but fools
do not imitate the successes of the wise.

Cato the Elder, From Plutarch, Lives

There is nothing so easy but that it becomes
difficult when you do it reluctantly.

Terence, Heauton Timoroumenos

The renown which riches or beauty confer is fleeting and
frail; mental excellence is a splendid and lasting possession.

Sallust, The War with Catiline

The splendid achievements of the intellect,
like the soul, are everlasting.

Sallust, The War with Jugurtha

Force without wisdom falls of its own weight.

Horace, Odes

Let a fool hold his tongue and he will pass for a sage.
Publilius Syrus, Maxim

What is hateful to you do not do to your neighbor. That is
the whole Torah. The rest is commentary.
Hillel, From Talmud

A good mind possesses a kingdom.
Lucius Annaeus Seneca, Thyestes

Beauty and wisdom are rarely conjoined.
Gaius Petronius, Satyricon

Those who wish to appear wise among fools,
among the wise seem foolish.
Quintilian, De Institutione Oratoria

What is the first business of one who practices philosophy?
To get rid of self-conceit. For it is impossible for anyone to
begin to learn that which he thinks he already knows.
Epictetus, Discourses

Three things are necessary for the salvation of man: to
know what he ought to believe; to know what he ought to
desire; and to know what he ought to do.
Saint Thomas Aquinas, Two Precepts of Charity

Reason in man is rather like God in the world.
Saint Thomas Aquinas, Opuscule 11, De Regno

In silence man can most readily preserve his integrity.
Meister Eckhart, Directions for the Contemplative Life

One must not always think so much about what one should
do, but rather what one should be. Our works do not
ennoble us; but we must ennoble our works.
Meister Eckhart, Work and Being

The gretteste clerkes been noght the wisest men.
Geoffrey Chaucer, The Canterbury Tales

Ah God! Had I but studied
In the days of my foolish youth.
François Villon, Le Grand Testament

The greatest thing in the world is to
know how to belong to oneself.
Michel Eyquem de Montaigne, Essays

Knowledge is power.
Francis Bacon, Meditationes Sacrae

They are ill discoverers that think there is no land,
when they can see nothing but sea.

Francis Bacon, The Advancement of Learning

The fool doth think he is wise, but the wise
man knows himself to be a fool.

William Shakespeare, As You Like It

All we know is still infinitely less than
all that still remains unknown.

William Harvey, De Motu Cordis et Sanguinis

It is not enough to have a good mind.
The main thing is to use it well.

René Descartes, Le Discours de la Méthode

Where there is much desire to learn, there of necessity will
be much arguing, much writing, many opinions; for
opinion in good men is but knowledge in the making.

John Milton, Areopagitica

Authority without wisdom is like a heavy axe without
an edge, fitter to bruise than polish.

Anne Bradstreet, Meditations Divine and Moral

The only fence against the world is a
thorough knowledge of it.

John Locke, Some Thoughts Concerning Education

All men think all men mortal but themselves.

Edward Young, Night Thoughts

For fools rush in where angels fear to tread.

Alexander Pope, An Essay on Criticism

You have to study a great deal to know a little.

Charles de Secondat, Baron de Montesquieu,
Pensées et Fragments Inédits de Montesquieu

The knowledge of the world is only to be acquired
in the world, and not in a closet.

Philip Dormer Stanhope, Earl of Chesterfield, Letters to His Son

Wear your learning, like your watch, in a private pocket:
and do not pull it out and strike it, merely to
show that you have one.

Philip Dormer Stanhope, Earl of Chesterfield, Letters to His Son

Liberty of thought is the life of the soul.

Voltaire, Essay on Epic Poetry

A word to the wise is enough, and many
words won't fill a bushel.

Benjamin Franklin, Poor Richard's Almanac

Genius is nothing but a greater aptitude for patience.

Georges Louis Leclerc de Buffon, Attributed

What wisdom can you find that is greater than kindness?

Jean-Jacques Rousseau, Emile; or, On Education

A man should know something of his own country, too,
before he goes abroad.

Laurence Sterne, Tristram Shandy

Great thoughts come from the heart.

Luc de Clapiers, Marquis de Vauvenargues, Réflexions et Maximes

Superstition is the religion of feeble minds.

Edmund Burke, Reflections on the Revolution in France

He who doesn't lose his wits over certain
things has no wits to lose.

Gotthold Ephraim Lessing, Emilia Galotti

A fool must now and then be right, by chance.

William Cowper, Conversation

Knowledge is proud that he has learn'd so much;
Wisdom is humble that he knows no more.

William Cowper, The Task

Let every sluice of knowledge be opened and set a-flowing.

John Adams, A Dissertation on the Canon and Feudal Law

What wise or stupid thing can man conceive
That was not thought of in ages long ago?

Johann Wolfgang von Goethe, Faust

Doubt grows with knowledge.

Johann Wolfgang von Goethe, Proverbs in Prose

All intelligent thoughts have already been thought; what is
necessary is only to try to think them again.

Johann Wolfgang von Goethe, Proverbs in Prose

In idle wishes fools supinely stay;
Be there a will, and wisdom finds a way.

George Crabbe, The Birth of Flattery

The road of excess leads to the palace of wisdom.
William Blake, The Marriage of Heaven and Hell

What you don't know would make a great book.
Sydney Smith, Lady Holland's Memoir

Sorrow is knowledge: they who know the most
Must mourn the deepest o'er the fatal truth,
The Tree of Knowledge is not that of Life.
George Noel Gordon, Lord Byron, Manfred

Nothing ever becomes real till it is experienced — Even a
proverb is no Proverb to you till your Life has illustrated it.
John Keats, Letter to George and Georgiana Keats

Meek young men grow up in libraries, believing it their
duty to accept the views which Cicero, which Locke,
which Bacon have given, forgetful that Cicero, Locke
and Bacon were only young men in libraries
when they wrote these books.
Ralph Waldo Emerson, The American Scholar

Nothing astonishes men so much as
common sense and plain dealing.
Ralph Waldo Emerson, Essays

What is a weed? A plant whose virtues
have not yet been discovered.

Ralph Waldo Emerson, Fortune of the Republic

Less is more.

Robert Browning, Andrea del Sarto

Let sleeping dogs lie — who wants to rouse 'em?

Charles Dickens, David Copperfield

There is a wisdom of the head, and . . .
a wisdom of the heart.

Charles Dickens, Hard Times

To be a philosopher is not merely to have subtle thoughts,
nor even to found a school, but so to love wisdom as to
live accordingly to its dictates, a life of simplicity,
independence, magnanimity, and trust.

Henry David Thoreau, Walden

Axiom: hatred of the bourgeois is the beginning of wisdom.

Gustave Flaubert, Letter to George Sand

Nothing in education is so astonishing as the amount of
ignorance it accumulates in the form of inert facts.

Henry Adams, The Education of Henry Adams

The art of being wise is the art of
knowing what to overlook.

William James, The Principles of Psychology

Sometimes a cigar is just a cigar.

Sigmund Freud, Attributed

Education is not preparation for life; education is life itself.

John Dewey, Attributed

Scepticism is the chastity of the intellect, and it is shameful
to surrender it too soon or to the first comer.

George Santayana, Scepticism and Animal Faith

I keep six honest serving men
(They taught me all I knew);
Their names are What and Why and When
And How and Where and Who.

Rudyard Kipling, The Just-So Stories

We prove what we want to prove, and the real difficulty
is to know what we want to prove.

Émile Auguste Chartier, Système des Beaux-Arts

Nothing is more dangerous than an idea,
when it's the only one we have.

Émile Auguste Chartier, Libres-propos

Omit needless words.

William Strunk Jr., The Elements of Style

Fear is the main source of superstition, and one of
the main sources of cruelty. To conquer
fear is the beginning of wisdom.

Bertrand Russell, Earl Russell, An Outline of Intellectual Rubbish

The history of every country begins in
the heart of a man or a woman.

Willa Cather, O Pioneers!

I shall be telling this with a sigh
Somewhere ages and ages hence:
Two roads diverged in a wood, and I —
I took the one less traveled by,
And that has made all the difference.

Robert Frost, The Road Not Taken

The older I grow the more I distrust the
familiar doctrine that age brings wisdom.

H. L. Mencken, Prejudices

The only wisdom we can hope to acquire
Is the wisdom of humility: humility is endless.

T. S. Eliot, Four Quartets

God, give us grace to accept with serenity the things that
cannot be changed, courage to change the things
which should be changed, and the wisdom
to distinguish the one from the other.

Reinhold Niebuhr, The Serenity Prayer

It is better to know some of the questions
than all of the answers.

James Thurber, Saying

Ninety-nine percent of the people in the world are fools
and the rest of us are in great danger of contagion.

Thornton Wilder, The Matchmaker

It is only with the heart that one can see rightly;
what is essential is invisible to the eye.

Antoine de Saint-Exupéry, The Little Prince

The longest journey
Is the journey inwards
Of him who has chosen his destiny.

Dag Hammarskjöld, Markings

We know the human brain is a device to keep
the ears from grating on one another.

Peter De Vries, Comfort Me with Apples

So it goes.

Kurt Vonnegut, Slaughterhouse-Five

Wisdom is not bought.

Anonymous, African proverb

Work and Success

Follow your desire as long as you live and do not perform
more than is ordered; do not lessen the time of following
desire, for the wasting of time is an abomination to the
spirit. . . . When riches are gained, follow desire,
for riches will not profit if one is sluggish.

Ptahhotpe, The Maxims of Ptahhotpe

Remember the sabbath day, to keep it holy.
Six days shalt thou labor, and do all thy work:
But the seventh day thou shalt not do any work.

The Bible, The Second Book of Moses, Called Exodus

Lead me to the rock that is higher than I.

The Bible, The Book of Psalms

Where there is no vision, the people perish.

The Bible, The Proverbs

Seek not out the things that are too hard for thee, neither
search the things that are above thy strength.

*The Bible, The Apocrypha, The Wisdom of Jesus
the Son of Sirach, or Ecclesiasticus*

Observe the opportunity.

The Bible, The Apocrypha, The Wisdom of Jesus
the Son of Sirach, or Ecclesiasticus

Be not overwise in doing thy business.

The Bible, The Apocrypha, The Wisdom of Jesus
the Son of Sirach, or Ecclesiasticus

Many are called, but few are chosen.

The Bible, Matthew

Do not count your chickens before they are hatched.

Aesop, The Milkmaid and Her Pail

Slow and steady wins the race.

Aesop, The Hare and the Tortoise

Haste in every business brings failures.

Herodotus, Histories

Give me where to stand, and I will move the earth.

Archimedes, From Pappus of Alexandria, Collectio

No sooner said than done — so acts your man of worth.

Quintus Ennius, Annals

I would much rather have men ask why I have no statue,
than why I have one.

Cato the Elder, From Plutarch, Lives

I came, I saw, I conquered.

Julius Caesar, From Suetonius, Lives of the Caesars

Talk of nothing but business,
and dispatch that business quickly.

Aldus Manutius, Placard on the door of the Aldine Press, Venice

Shun those studies in which the work
that results dies with the worker.

Leonardo da Vinci, The Notebooks

Many hands make light work.

John Heywood, Proverbs

Ill can he rule the great, that cannot reach the small.

Edmund Spenser, The Faerie Queene

If a man will begin with certainties, he shall end in doubts;
but if he will be content to begin with doubts
he shall end in certainties.

Francis Bacon, The Advancement of Learning

He that will not apply new remedies must expect new evils;
for time is the greatest innovator.

Francis Bacon, Essays

No profit grows where is no pleasure ta'en;
In brief, sir, study what you most affect.

William Shakespeare, The Taming of the Shrew

Superfluity comes sooner by white hairs,
but competency lives longer.

William Shakespeare, The Merchant of Venice

We cannot all be masters.

William Shakespeare, Othello

A dwarf standing on the shoulders of a giant
may see farther than a giant himself.

Robert Burton, The Anatomy of Melancholy

By labor and intent study (which I take to be my portion in
this life), joined with the strong propensity of nature,
I might perhaps leave something so written to
after-times, as they should not willingly let it die.

John Milton, The Reason of Church Government

Knowledge may give weight, but accomplishments give
luster, and many more people see than weigh.

Philip Dormer Stanhope, Earl of Chesterfield, Letters to His Son

Work keeps us from three great evils,
boredom, vice, and poverty.

Voltaire, Candide

Discipline is the soul of an army. It makes small numbers
formidable; procures success to the weak, and esteem to all.

*George Washington, Letter of Instructions
to the Captains of the Virginia Regiments*

A dinner lubricates business.

William Scott, Lord Stowell, From Boswell, Life of Johnson

One must be something to be able to do something.

*Johann Wolfgang von Goethe, Conversation
with Johann Peter Eckermann*

The deed is everything, the glory nothing.

Johann Wolfgang von Goethe, Faust

Never say more than is necessary.

Richard Brinsley Sheridan, The Rivals

You will find it a very good practice always
to verify your references, sir.

Martin Joseph Routh, From J. W. Burgon, Memoir of Dr. Routh

No bird soars too high, if he soars with his own wings.

William Blake, The Marriage of Heaven and Hell

He who has done his best for his own
time has lived for all times.

Johann Friedrich von Schiller, Wallenstein's Camp

Who reflects too much will accomplish little.

Johann Friedrich von Schiller, Wilhelm Tell

We may affirm absolutely that nothing great in the world
has been accomplished without passion.

Georg Wilhelm Friedrich Hegel, Philosophy of History

We never do anything well till we cease to
think about the manner of doing it.

William Hazlitt, Sketches and Essay

All work is as seed sown; it grows and spreads,
and sows itself anew.

Thomas Carlyle, On Boswell's Life of Johnson

All work, even cotton spinning, is noble; work is alone
noble. . . . A life of ease is not for any man, nor for any god.
Thomas Carlyle, Past and Present

Great blunders are often made, like large ropes,
of a multitude of fibers.
Victor Hugo, Les Misérables

All that Adam had, all that Caesar could, you have and
can do. . . . Build, therefore, your own world.
Ralph Waldo Emerson, Nature

Make yourself necessary to somebody.
Ralph Waldo Emerson, The Conduct of Life

The secret of success is constancy to purpose.
Benjamin Disraeli, Earl of Beaconsfield, Speech

Ah, but a man's reach should exceed his grasp,
Or what's a heaven for?
Robert Browning, Andrea del Sarto

A minute's success pays the failure of years.
Robert Browning, Apollo and the Fates

My guiding star always is, Get hold of portable property.
Charles Dickens, Great Expectations

Our ideas are only intellectual instruments which we use
to break into phenomena; we must change them when they
have served their purpose, as we change a blunt lancet
that we have used long enough.
Claude Bernard, Introduction à l'Étude de la Médecine Expérimentale

In the long run men hit only what they aim at.
Henry David Thoreau, Walden

If one advances confidently in the direction of his dreams,
and endeavors to live the life which he has imagined, he
will meet with a success unexpected in common hours.
Henry David Thoreau, Walden

When commercial capital occupies a position of
unquestioned ascendancy, it everywhere
constitutes a system of plunder.
Karl Marx, Capital

There is no better ballast for keeping the mind steady on its
keel, and saving it from all risk of crankiness, than business.
James Russell Lowell, Literary Essays

Business? It's quite simple. It's other people's money.
Alexandre Dumas the Younger, La Question d'Argent

Work consists of whatever a body is obliged to do. . . . Play
consists of whatever a body is not obliged to do.
Mark Twain, The Adventures of Tom Sawyer

Thunder is good, thunder is impressive; but it is the
lightning that does the work.
Mark Twain, Letter to an Unidentified Person

Success depends on three things: who says it, what he says,
how he says it; and of these three things,
what he says is the least important.
John, Viscount Morley of Blackburn, Recollections

Man is so made that he can only find relaxation from
one kind of labor by taking up another.
Anatole France, The Crime of Sylvestre Bonnard

There is only one thing in the world worse than being
talked about, and that is not being talked about.
Oscar Wilde, The Picture of Dorian Gray

Experience is the name everyone gives to their mistakes.
Oscar Wilde, Lady Windermere's Fan

He who can, does. He who cannot, teaches.
George Bernard Shaw, Man and Superman

Never give a sucker an even break.
Edward F. Albee, Remark

I don't like work — no man does — but I like what is in
work — the chance to find yourself. Your own reality —
for yourself, not for others — what no other
man can ever know.
Joseph Conrad, Heart of Darkness

You may tempt the upper classes
With your villainous demitasses,
But Heaven will protect the working girl.
Edgar Smith, Heaven Will Protect the Working Girl

I wish to preach, not the doctrine of ignoble ease,
but the doctrine of the strenuous life.
Theodore Roosevelt, Speech before the Hamilton Club, Chicago

I like work: it fascinates me. I can sit and look at it
for hours. I love to keep it by me; the idea of getting
rid of it nearly breaks my heart.

Jerome K. Jerome, Three Men in a Boat

An expert is one who knows more and
more about less and less.

Nicholas Murray Butler, Commencement address, Columbia University

The most decisive actions of our life . . .
are most often unconsidered actions.

André Gide, Les Faux Monnayeurs (The Counterfeiters)

He has achieved success who has lived well, laughed often
and loved much; who has enjoyed the trust of pure
women and the love of little children; who has
filled his niche and accomplished his task; who has
left the world better than he found it, whether by an
improved poppy, a perfect poem, or a rescued soul;
who has never lacked appreciation of earth's beauty or
failed to express it; who has always looked for the best in
others and given them the best he had; whose life was
an inspiration; whose memory a benediction.

Bessie Anderson Stanley, Success

A jackass can kick a barn down,
but it takes a carpenter to build one.

Sam Rayburn, Remark

Once a decision was made,
I did not worry about it afterward.

Harry S. Truman, Memoirs

The buck stops here.

Harry S. Truman, Sign on Truman's desk when President

Where I was born and where and how I have lived is
unimportant. It is what I have done with where
I have been that should be of interest.

Georgia O'Keeffe, Georgia O'Keeffe

Sometimes, however, to be a "ruined man"
is itself a vocation.

T. S. Eliot, The Use of Poetry and the Use of Criticism

There's no such thing as a free lunch.

Milton Friedman, Attributed

The struggle to reach the top is itself enough to fulfill the
heart of man. One must believe that Sisyphus is happy.

Albert Camus, The Myth of Sisyphus

High school is closer to the core of the American
experience than anything else I can think of.

Kurt Vonnegut, From his introduction to Our Time Is Now: Notes from
the High School Underground, *edited by John Birmingham*

Power is the great aphrodisiac.

Henry Kissinger, In the New York Times

Eighty percent of success is showing up.

Woody Allen, Interview

Today is the first day of the rest of your life.

Anonymous, Wall slogan

Youth and Aging

Our days on the earth are as a shadow.
The Bible, The First Book of the Chronicles

Cast me not off in the time of old age;
forsake me not when my strength faileth.
The Bible, The Book of Psalms

Despise not thy mother when she is old.
The Bible, The Proverbs

Rejoice, O young man, in thy youth.
The Bible, Ecclesiastes; or, The Preacher

It is good for a man that he bear the yoke in his youth.
The Bible, The Lamentations of Jeremiah

No man loves life like him that's growing old.
Sophocles, Acrisius, fragment

Old men are children for a second time.

Aristophanes, Clouds

Give me a young man in whom there is something of the
old, and an old man with something of the young: guided
so, a man may grow old in body, but never in mind.

Marcus Tullius Cicero, De Senectute

Grant me, sound of body and of mind, to pass an
old age lacking neither honor nor the lyre.

Horace, Odes

If only, when one heard
That Old Age was coming
One could bolt the door,
Answer "Not at home"
And refuse to meet him!

Anonymous, Kokinshu (Collection of Ancient and Modern Poems)

But, Lord Crist! whan that it remembreth me
Upon my yowthe, and on my jolitee,
It tikleth me aboute myn herte roote.
Unto this day it dooth myn herte boote
That I have had my world as in my tyme.

Geoffrey Chaucer, The Canterbury Tales

As a well-spent day brings happy sleep,
so life well used brings happy death.

Leonardo da Vinci, The Notebooks

There is no fool to the old fool.

John Heywood, Proverbs

Live now, believe me, wait not till tomorrow;
Gather the roses of life today.

Pierre de Ronsard, Sonnets pour Hélène

Harvest, oh! harvest your hour
While life is abloom with youth!
For age with bitter ruth
Will fade your beauty's flower.

Pierre de Ronsard, Odes

Young men think old men are fools;
but old men know young men are fools.

George Chapman, All Fools

Alonso of Aragon was wont to say in commendation of age,
that age appears to be best in four things — old wood
best to burn, old wine to drink, old friends to trust,
and old authors to read.

Francis Bacon, Apothegms

My comfort is, that old age, that ill layer-up of beauty,
can do no more spoil upon my face.

William Shakespeare, King Henry the Fifth

Men must endure
Their going hence, even as their coming hither:
Ripeness is all.

William Shakespeare, King Lear

Thou art thy mother's glass, and she in thee
Calls back the lovely April of her prime.

William Shakespeare, Sonnet 3

What's past is prologue.

William Shakespeare, The Tempest

Is not old wine wholesomest, old pippins toothsomest, old
wood burn brightest, old linen wash whitest? Old soldiers,
sweethearts, are surest, and old lovers are soundest.

John Webster, Westward Hoe

Youth is the time of getting, middle age of improving,
and old age of spending.

Anne Bradstreet, Meditations Divine and Moral

Life is an incurable disease.

Abraham Cowley, To Dr. Scarborough

It is a man's own fault, it is from want of use,
if his mind grows torpid in old age.

Samuel Johnson, From Boswell, Life of Johnson

But though an old man, I am but a young gardener.

Thomas Jefferson, Letter to Charles Willson Peale

Age does not make us childish, as they say.
It only finds us true children still.

Johann Wolfgang von Goethe, Faust

Once a man's thirty, he's already old,
He is indeed as good as dead.
It's best to kill him right away.

Johann Wolfgang von Goethe, Faust

We do not count a man's years until he
has nothing else to count.

Ralph Waldo Emerson, Society and Solitude

In youth men are apt to write more wisely than they really
know or feel; and the remainder of life may be not
idly spent in realizing and convincing themselves of
the wisdom which they uttered long ago.

Nathaniel Hawthorne, The Snow Image

There is no time like the old time,
when you and I were young.

Oliver Wendell Holmes, No Time Like the Old Time

I have come too late into a world too old.

Alfred de Musset, Rolla

Why stay we on the earth except to grow?

Robert Browning, Cleon

Was your youth of pleasure wasteful?
Mine I saved and hold complete.
Do your joys with age diminish?
When mine fail me, I'll complain.
Must in death your daylight finish?
My sun sets to rise again.

Robert Browning, At the "Mermaid"

The youth gets together his materials to build a bridge
to the moon, or, perchance, a palace or temple on the
earth, and, at length, the middle-aged man
concludes to build a woodshed with them.

Henry David Thoreau, Journal

There is no hopelessness so sad as that of early youth,
when the soul is made up of wants, and has no long
memories, no superadded life in the life of others.

George Eliot, The Mill on the Floss

When all the world is young, lad,
And all the trees are green;
And every goose a swan, lad,
And every lass a queen;
Then hey for boot and horse, lad,
And round the world away:
Young blood must have its course, lad,
And every dog his day.

Charles Kingsley, Water Babies

To know how to grow old is the masterwork of wisdom,
and one of the most difficult chapters in
the great art of living.

Henri-Frédéric Amiel, Journal Intime

Young men have a passion for regarding
their elders as senile.

Henry Adams, The Education of Henry Adams

Young man, the secret of my success is that at an
early age I discovered I was not God.

Oliver Wendell Holmes Jr.,
Reply to a reporter's question on his ninetieth birthday

We hold the period of youth sacred to education, and the
period of maturity, when the physical forces begin to flag,
equally sacred to ease and agreeable relaxation.

Edward Bellamy, Looking Backward

Youth is wholly experimental.

Robert Louis Stevenson, Letter to a Young Gentleman

There is no cure for birth and
death save to enjoy the interval.

George Santayana, Soliloquies in England and Later Soliloquies

The young man who has not wept is a savage,
and the old man who will not laugh is a fool.

George Santayana, Dialogues in Limbo

We don't understand life any better at forty than
at twenty, but we know it and admit it.

Jules Renard, Journal

There is more felicity on the far side of baldness
than young men can possibly imagine.

Logan Pearsall Smith, Afterthoughts

Older men declare war. But it is youth that must fight and
die. And it is youth who must inherit the tribulation, the
sorrow, and the triumphs that are the aftermath of war.

Herbert Hoover, Speech at the Republican National Convention, Chicago

As a white candle
In a holy place,
So is the beauty
Of an aged face.

Joseph Campbell, The Old Woman

All lovely things will have an ending,
All lovely things will fade and die,
And youth, that's now so bravely spending,
Will beg a penny by and by.

Conrad Aiken, All Lovely Things

My candle burns at both ends;
It will not last the night;
But, ah, my foes, and, oh, my friends —
It gives a lovely light.

Edna St. Vincent Millay, A Few Figs from Thistles

Grown-ups never understand anything for themselves,
and it is tiresome for children to be always and
forever explaining things to them.

Antoine de Saint-Exupéry, The Little Prince

Here lies my past. Good-bye I have kissed it;
Thank you, kids. I wouldn't have missed it.

Ogden Nash, You Can't Get There from Here

There is always one moment in childhood when
the door opens and lets the future in.

Graham Greene, The Power and the Glory

About 60 years ago, I said to my father, "Old Mr. Senex is
showing his age; he sometimes talks quite stupidly."
My father replied, "That isn't age. He's always been stupid.
He is just losing his ability to conceal it."

*Robertson Davies, You're Not Getting Older, You're Getting Nosier, in the
New York Times Book Review*

Do not go gentle into that good night,
Old age should burn and rave at close of day;
Rage, rage against the dying of the light.

Dylan Thomas, Do Not Go Gentle into That Good Night

The young need old men. They need men who are
not ashamed of age, not pathetic imitations of
themselves. . . . Parents are the bones on
which children sharpen their teeth.

Peter Ustinov, Dear Me

Knowing who you are is good for one generation only.

Flannery O'Connor, Everything That Rises Must Converge

When you know your name, you should hang on to it,
for unless it is noted down and remembered,
it will die when you do.

Toni Morrison, Song of Solomon

Index